Memoir of Po...

goalkeeper

Games
secrets
epilepsy
& love

SPONDYLUXPRESS

Published October 2021 in the UK by Spondylux Press.

Edited by N.E. McMorran
Co-editor Catalina Gutiérrez

Cover design © Spondylux Press 2021
Author portrait © John Bentley
Photographs courtesy Peter Street
P 186 © *The Bolton News* (formerly *Bolton Evening News*)
P 92 © *Bolton Wanderers FC*

This is a work of non-fiction, with events portrayed to the best of
the author's memory. While all the stories are true, some names
and identifying details have been changed to protect privacy.

ISBN: 978-1-8380978-3-7 (print)
ISBN: 978-1-8380978-7-5 (e-book)

A CIP catalogue record for this title is available from the British Library.

Printed and bound by CPI Group (UK) Ltd, Croydon CR0 4YY,
using sustainably sourced, manufactured and FSC certified Enso paper.

Peter Street is a British autistic author and poet, born in Wigan, 1948. He has published five poetry collections and performed his work internationally on television and radio, including BBC Manchester where he was poet in residence. He won a National Poetry Society commission and wrote a series of poems in collaboration with fine artist Tony Bevan.

Street was a Royal Literary Fund recipient and has been writer in residence in schools, colleges and prisons. He is also a qualified youth worker, and previously worked as a chef, head gardener, gravedigger and exhumer.

Peter was diagnosed with epilepsy at fifteen, and, fifty years later, after returning from war-torn Croatia with PTSD, received his formal autism diagnosis at the age of sixty-six. He lives with his wife Sandra, and has two children and six grandchildren.

Follow Peter on Twitter *@peterstreet339*

To Mum and Dad,
who gave up everything for me.

Acknowledgements

Thanks to my wife Sandra, for her reading and feedback, Lorriane Worsley, Ged O'Brien and Matt Simpson for their guidance and advice, Spondylux Press and editor N.E. McMorran for their patience and support in developing Goalkeeper for publication. And last, but not least, Bolton and England goalkeeper Eddie Hopkinson for his inspiration.

Foreword

Lorraine Worsley-Carter MBE DL

I met Peter Street in the late eighties. He had written a book of poems and I thought he would make an interesting guest for my then BBC Radio Manchester programme. I remember Peter coming into the studio: I was struck by his openness, his almost childlike candour, and his tangible wonder at being in front of a microphone live on air. He did himself proud.

Peter became something of a regular on the programme. He would talk about the now late Poet Laureate Ted Hughes, of whom I knew little apart from the name. Peter soon rectified this.

Peter was obviously a 'local lad' to Greater Manchester, proud of his roots, steadfast in his craft, holder of a wicked sense of humour behind twinkling eyes. He was of indeterminate age, a bit of a Peter Pan, and we became friends. He spoke of his 'rock' wife Sandra, but little else about his background. This didn't matter to me as I was more interested in having a poet on the programme!

It was evident that Peter was a welcome contributor to

the programme, much liked by the listeners, and I decided to have a word with a colleague working in a different department to me about the possibility of Peter becoming a 'Poet in Residence'. As far as I knew, this had never happened on a BBC local radio station, and I was all for innovation. I am sure my colleague worked very hard for this to happen, because I was delighted to be told that she had secured six months' funding.

I suppose I can honestly say that the rest is history. Peter embraced and enhanced the role and was soon doing all sorts of things for other parts of the BBC.

Media is adroit and fleeting: I moved on to other projects for my programme, and Peter and I lost touch. So I was thrilled when he contacted me again a few years ago and we met up for a coffee. It was a very long coffee break at the Lowry Theatre in Salford Quays as he relayed his travels, experiences and adventures. It was at that meeting that he told me about his recent autism diagnosis and how, suddenly, his life in the 1950s and onwards made perfect sense to him and gave him peace.

I had never realised that Peter was on the autism spectrum, nor the fact that he was an accomplished sportsman, and was fascinated to hear more. He told me that one day he would '*write a book about those early memories: the light and the shade, the heart break, the bullying, the pain, and the smiles*'. I am overjoyed that he has done so.

1

MANCHESTER 1993

A local newspaper was calling for volunteers to help load the biggest ever humanitarian aid convoy. An effort organised by the police and fire brigades of England to mobilise dozens of HGVs, vans, and a fully equipped fire engine gifted by East Midlands Fire Service to the Croatian village of Lipik, which had been bombed out of all recognition.

I invited two police officers into BBC Greater Manchester Radio, where I was, at the time, poet in residence. Live on air, Sergeant John explained they would be taking desperately needed aid to war-torn Croatia and expressed concern for single mothers, with very young children who had little chance of seeing their birth fathers; even less of finding somewhere safe and permanent to live. He stressed the need for volunteers to help load aid onto the many wagons.

My mouth gave no warning to my brain when it suddenly let out, "Can I hitch a lift?"

There was a short, stunned silence before he responded with, "We leave in six weeks. Can you be ready?"

"I'll be ready."

My wife, Sandra, wasn't immediately on board. "What about your epilepsy—what happens if you're ill?"

Trying to convince her with, "There'll be medics and nurses," didn't wash.

"Disabled people come *back* from a war," she exclaimed. "They don't go to war. You can't cope with the Hoover, never mind the sounds of war. You get lost everywhere you go. And who'll sort your tablets?"

It was silent meals for almost six weeks.

Sandra fastened 'Harry', my six-inch teddy bear, to the straps of my rucksack. Tears welling. It was then I realised I had hurt her.

"No," she said, sensing my hesitation. "It's too late, you can't back out now."

All my words were bunched together in a big ball, stinging my throat, too tight to escape. My rucksack leapt onto my back, and, together, we pushed our way through the front door.

Inside the taxi, I forced myself to look back at the front window. She wasn't there. I tried the bedroom window. No sign.

I waved to our house, and that was it. I was on my way.

***

Watching the white cliffs of Dover slide away from us, there was a strange sense of anticipation I couldn't quite understand.

On the ferry, I was already being called out for wandering off from the main party of officers, medics, and volunteers. When the ferry swayed, I swear I saw handguns under the jackets of some men dressed in ordinary clothes.

We were soon in Europe. Our first resting stop was on the autobahns in Germany. I was doing okay until my *smells* came back and the stench of something between urine and burnt coffee smacked my nose. It didn't seem to be affecting the others. Everyone sat on the grass, a hundred yards from the convoy, in their own groups. Talking, killing their fags, but not showing any emotion: fear, whatever. I had the sudden urge to get away. The realisation had hit, more than any other moment in my life: I wasn't one of the herd. I was *me*.

A red-haired woman came over to chat. She was friendly, asking where I was from and who I was with. I boasted about being a poet. She talked Ted Hughes and I talked Charles Causley. It was okay while it was just her, but when half a dozen of her friends came over too, I started feeling full-up of people.

Slovenian-Croatian border

In the far distance, artillery was pounding poor souls and their surroundings. I stood there, alone in the middle of two hundred people, as we all watched in silence. My body and I felt strange. Deeper than an ordinary tingle, turning into a shudder, with a tankful of fright thrown in for good measure. After some army rations were finished off and fags killed, we were back on the road.

Our base camp for the next days was in the huge grounds of an international hotel just outside of Zagreb. Among the refugees was a mother, thinner than thin, holding a small child whilst pushing a battered pram with different-sized wheels and a bag full of pigswill swinging from its handlebars. Some of the refugees were literally dying on their feet. My mind flashed to 1948 and Mum, a single mother with me in tow, having to find a roof to put over our heads.

One of the men from the ferry began shouting at me for giving my water and sterilising tablets to a mother laying on the ground. "You're putting us all at risk!" I thought he was going to get hold of me when he leant in and added, "*Think* before you *do anything*! If you're unsure, *ask*." He then disappeared into the crowd.

Meanwhile, a Scottish journalist was swearing at the distraught woman pushing the battered pram. He was telling her to get away and stop pestering him, when some copper warned him to mind his ways: "She's just pushed her children through thirty miles of war zone!..."

The journalist only shrugged his shoulders, as though nothing mattered to him, and lay back down on the warm grass. Two other coppers I didn't recognise took the bag of pigswill from her and exchanged it for rice, pasta, flour and a dozen packets of army rations.

Another refugee in a similar state, with babies in tow, was close behind. I gave her ten Deutsche Marks, a tin of pilchards, and a bag of rice. She dropped to her knees, crying at my feet. The woman with the red hair from our convoy helped the woman across the grass and gave her some more money. They hugged.

Hours later, it was the drive into Zagreb towards our first refugee camp. There we saw mothers at the roadside holding up their babies for us to take them to safety, we assumed. It was at that moment my eyes hit a dog being knocked down and a young woman, like a duck in a shooting range, chancing her luck to dodge the traffic and take up the dead dog. She humped it back over the road and into an empty pram, where her friend was waiting with a baby in her arms. I pointed for everyone to look, but no one took any notice. Perhaps it hadn't been enough to bother them. But it *had me*.

Half a mile down the fast road turned us into the camp to deliver food and cooking equipment. Our wagons rocked and jerked through lines of potholes where we sank foot-deep into a make-do cinder path. All alongside us, children were walking barefoot. It was a ride into something I didn't understand. Yards ahead, a fire had almost finished burning a pile of old rags, and the ribcage of something I couldn't quite recognise. To our right, shelters not much bigger than those I used to see when visiting the local cats and dogs' home. There were mothers fiddling around for whatever bits of food they could find. Some were washing their hair and arms, while children close by were coughing loud, barking coughs. Naked kids close to the taps were splashing water into mud pies. It was there that a very dark brown stench started to bash my nose, and, yes, there was something human about it.

A young man, maybe twenty years old, was pushing his way through a group of women toward me. We came face to face as he introduced himself. "Josip. My name is Josip." A week or so before we hit that camp had been his birthday. Whilst visiting a friend's house further down the village, his own house had suffered a direct hit, with all his family and friends inside. He had no one left except those in the refugee camp.

His English was very good and he offered to be my translator. I accepted. From his tattered jacket pocket, Josip took out his only possession: a book of Percy Shelley poems. He showed me around the camp and we tried to talk with some of the young people, but, even with the help of my young translator, they seemed too traumatised to speak. Many started crying as we approached them. I followed Josip into a building where there were lines of bunk beds, few with mattresses on them—the local Mafia had been in and stolen them, then offered to sell them back to the villagers, but no one had had any money. Outside the building, mothers were trying to sort everything to keep their kids alive and clean, while the men, squat against the wall, were begging cigarettes for themselves.

I thought I had experienced the worst of human stench, but this was something different. This was *way* beyond the cocktail of sulphur and diarrhoea I was hit with gravedigging and exhuming, way back in my late teens. I wanted to be back down in a seven-foot grave where life and death was much simpler, and fun. Like the time we lowered the coffin of a brass band member into a grave and accidentally flooded it after hitting an underground stream, the water bringing him straight back up as the band played 'Shall We Gather at the River'.

Lipik: 76 miles from Zagreb

Karlovac had become far too dangerous, with all the shelling and heavy machine gun fire, so it was decided we head to Lipik instead, where, around eighteen months before, Colonel Cook and the British Army had promised to help the village rebuild their school and orphanage.

Steps were striding me, along with several ounces of anticipation, up into the cab of an HGV full of aid. The copper driving it introduced himself as Paul.

"I'm Peter."

"All we need now is a 'Mary'," he said with a smile.

We shook hands as air horns stood up and screamed *GO*! And that was it, I was in a convoy.

We hit the countryside, driving past gardens full of plum trees waving back at us. Soon we were in Lipik and hit with the first evidence of war: a police station with its face blown off. A plague of journalists took over the buildings of the little town, going in and out of everywhere and everything, regardless of the residents. Steel girders that had held up buildings were now bent and knotted together in strange, alien shapes. There were fragments of burnt glass everywhere we trod, crunching over the blown-in windows. There had been fires caused by the bombing. Temperatures way beyond anything my father experienced down in the 'fire-hole' and those six giant, coal-fired, cotton mill furnaces.

Two days later, a sixty-odd mile drive through wild countryside took us to the train station at Cakovec on the Croatian-Hungarian border. Old, broken-down train carriages stuffed with Muslim men, women, and children.

I spotted a young boy, maybe four years old, crawling under the carriages, and followed him to a single red-haired woman gripping a smaller boy with jet black hair. After informing the convoy, her carriage was immediately filled with food and fresh water. I couldn't take my eyes off her rosary beads and a statue of the Sacred Heart; I crossed myself.

Once the convoy was emptied of aid, the lights of the wagons went on and I was about to climb in when the woman came running towards me, calling and waving something in the air. She hugged me and cried, gifting me a T-shirt with a picture of St. Joseph, patron saint of Croatia, printed on it.

The little boy, finally catching up with his mum, gripped her hand before she lifted him up into her arms. And that was when my childhood grabbed me and pulled me back to 1952 when my mother had given up her family, her town, and her friends, just to keep me safe from those who would gladly have had me aborted.

2

WIGAN 1948

28th March

Kitty was sitting at the dresser in the dimly lit bedroom she shared with her sister, Liz. There was a navy blue A-line dress laid out on the bed. My mum was clipping up her hair when Liz stormed in, "So, you're going, then?" She ignored her, sliding in the final clip. "I don't know what you're doing all this for. Nobody can be so hard up that they would want to dance with you."

It was three years, on V. E. night, since Kitty had visited The Empress Ballroom. The globe in the centre was sparkling over two dancers demonstrating the flamenco. It was the sexiest thing she had ever witnessed. She could feel herself blushing as the dancers' bodies touched and wrapped around each other. She couldn't take her eyes off the male dancer as he twisted and twirled. She had never seen such tight trousers on a man before. She blushed even more as she imagined him holding her tight, breasts squeezing into his chest, and those firm thighs pressing into her. She made the sign of the cross, *Oh, God, forgive me for my impure thoughts*.

Before leaving the dance floor, he approached her and asked for a date. She accepted a nice drive in the countryside north of Bolton.

Kitty's Diary

I was a piece of meat he just dropped off.
Never said a word.
Wasn't the man on that dance floor. Didn't know what was happening.

December 1948

Kitty's Diary

Shunned because I wouldn't take the pennyroyal.

Mum had planned to call me Gabriel or Noel—until Uncle Peter suddenly died a fortnight before she pushed me out into the hands of a Wigan midwife in Billinge Hospital on

Christmas morning—and renamed me Peter.

For three years, Mum would have to cope with loneliness and the name-calling from local women who didn't even know her to women in her own village with whom she had once shared nylons and lipstick. It all became too much, especially when they started shouting, "How's that little bastard of yours?"

August 1952

Thomas Edgar Street, fire stoker in the same Bolton cotton mill where Mum worked, approached her with a deal. He needed a live-in housekeeper: laundry, cooking, that sort of thing. Mum accepted, but on her own terms. Terms she pencilled on a rough piece of paper right there and then, sitting beside her bag of chips and cold pot of tea on the outside wall of the mill. Neither knew anything about the other, but it was one of those opportune moments and Mum grabbed it with both hands.

Moor Lane Bus Station, Bolton

An old man waved to us and came over. We shook hands. Our heavy suitcase banged his legs while walking us to the

bus for the ten-minute ride to 339 Blackburn Road.

Mum took in a deep breath. "No need to be frightened," said Mr. Street, flaring a match, "You'll be all right here."

Kitty's Diary
He stinks of fags.

Smoke mingled with the shadows as thirteen steps walked us upstairs. A dark rail gripped my hand. The landing was long; my heart was bumping.

Kitty's Diary
Bedroom's a nice size. King-size bed. Enamel washbasin on the chest of drawers. Coal fire. Oak wardrobe. Sash windows.
Better than nothing.

The wooden floorboards were creaking him out of the bedroom when suddenly he stopped to check the door lock. Without looking back, he stormed out of our room. Mum and I held our breaths as he crossed the landing back toward the stairs. Mum flopped on the bed where she hugged me. She was always hugging and apologising. A giant clock above a jeweller's shop across the road was telling Mum it was seven-thirty. It would always be seven-thirty.

Kitty's Diary

November 1952

*He WILL start putting his teeth in… I swear, I'll… Jesus,
he's filthy.*

There were only a few hours before Mum had to be
downstairs to prepare the first family meal.

The four-leaf, drop-down oak table was reading a Bolton
Evening newspaper while holding up a bottle of vinegar, salt
and pepper, a pot of tea, a milk bottle, and two empty pint
mugs. Mum waited, arms folded, as Thomas Edgar killed his
Woodbine. Without any warning, she shouted, "You aren't
to come to the table in a filthy state. I'm not having it."

There was a long silence until he took the hint. "It's been
a long time, sorry," he said, before heading off to wash his
arms.

Egg and chips was our first dinner. Mum was relaxed
until he said, "You'll pile the laundry neatly on the small
table outside my yellow bedroom door. And you're never to
enter. There'll be no excuses." She was getting her thoughts
together when he added, "You can wash my smalls in the
kitchen sink: that way you won't steam the house out."

Kitty's Diary

January 1953

I'll swing if he hurts Peter.

He'll have his washing done Saturday—like it or lump it.

The silence was banging way beyond comfortable as he swallowed his last bite before sparking up a Woodbine and informing Mum that our baths would be in front of the fire whilst he was out at work. He pointed to the sixpence on the mantelpiece—for the slipper baths, but only when it was really needed. She waited, hands on hips, wondering what was going to hit us next. He surprised us with a smile and told her to go down to Maxi's pawn shop on Blackburn Road and buy herself a wedding dress.

There were more Woodbines and mugs of tea with seven sugars, before insisting his bedsheets be ironed, nice and crisp. And the same for all his clothes, especially his stained undergarments. He broke the silence to stress, "My bedroom door will always be locked and you will never enter."

Kitty's Diary
Peter tried the yellow door again. He can't understand all the secrecy.

Thursday 22nd January 1953

It was a registry office marriage. Mum, being a devout Irish Catholic, didn't recognise it. But it's what Dad wanted. Yes, she wore the ring, but that was as far as it went. There were two witnesses: June and Abrahana—Mum's friend who'd escaped the Nazis with baby Rachel wrapped tight in her arms. Rachel was four years older than me, and we were soon to become the best of friends. It was odd, though, how Rachel never said which school she went to.

I had a wonderful childhood. Strange, but wonderful. Strange in the sense that Dad was nearly sixty years older than me. Stranger still was the lie Mum and Dad lived in his large four-bedroom Victorian house. To the outside world, they were an ordinary married couple with all the usual problems of a 1950s working-class household. *Wrong*. For a start, Mum was from an Irish-Catholic family, whose grandad had witnessed the burning of Cork by the Black and Tans in 1916. Dad, a flat-footed Englishman, was sent to work on the Dublin docks alongside the Black and Tans, whom he hated with a vengeance.

Michael Collins, Irish politics, and religion were only ever mentioned when Mum was out of the house. Except on one rare occasion when Dad wasn't working: "I hate Irish women, all those Irish bitches enticing British soldiers into the hay barns." It was the only time I saw him so angry. "Men from the Michael Collins brigade would be waiting for them."

3

DRAIN HOLE IN MY HEAD

1st September 1954, when cobbles walked me and Mum through overhanging shadows down the back of Blackburn Street toward school. Where I remembered so vividly that morning's conversation about the place I would spend the next six years of my young life. I was Mum's only child, which made me more resilient, unlike the kids with brothers and sisters they could always lean on.

All the other children, clones in maroon and grey school uniforms, were crying, some screaming. Being taken to the nursery just a couple of months after I was born, acclimatised me for everything school was about to throw at me. Being away from Mum never bothered me; I was never lonely. Yes, there were odd times when the nursery insisted I play with the other kids, but I was happier on my own, doing my own thing. It was the beginning of who I was and who I was going to be.

Five or six women by the school gates, gathered with their heads close enough to make me think they had all been glued together in one massive clump of hair, were glancing and pointing at Mum, shaking their heads and making obvious their tut-tutting as we walked past them across the concrete playground. A bouncing hundred or so kids, with a few skipping ropes and footballs thrown in for good measure. Mum walked us up to the front of the queue, ready for my first steps into a new adventure.

The stink of Dettol walked my class between the canary-coloured brick walls. From there, fifteen stone steps carried us up to a classroom where a big woman with red lipstick and chipmunk cheeks introduced us to the school and told what was expected of us. It wasn't long before we were moved into the main hall, where boys and girls, much taller and older, like stretched-out figures, stood in lines.

"No need for the sobbing," Teacher shouted at the class. "I *said, stop it*!" The silence, loud, until, "Peter Street, why are you smiling?" Tearful eyes were all over me as I wondered how she already knew my name. Her shouting didn't bother me, but the rest of the class seemed terrified.

It wasn't long before we were led from the big hall back out of school, and a rush of screams ran toward our waiting parents, already bent over, ready to comfort their children.

30

Mum was yards behind all the others, waving. She was pushing her way through to make a little corridor for me, when some woman said something loud enough for Mum to hear. Mum let go of my hand and pushed herself backwards into the women behind her, shouting, "No one calls my Peter a bastard!"

The following day, when schooling really kicked in, I held hands with a red-haired girl called Pauline, who I'd not seen before. It was a boy-girl thing. We were all led to meet the priest and nuns before being ushered into our permanent classroom to meet our teacher, the blonde Miss Norton.

A chubby, curly-haired boy called Robert tapped me on the shoulder and giggled, infecting the whole class before Teacher finally shouted for us to stop. Over milk break, Robert and I became instant friends, but, after all the trouble we had caused in the classroom, Miss Norton never let us sit next to each other ever again. Robert was one of maybe half a dozen kids who came to school in their parents' big, shiny cars, but none of the other kids would play with or even talk to him. With me, he would never stop talking, and his hands and knees had never enjoyed being so dirty. Not only that, but he had never circled the toilet peeing in the same bowl with a friend, or ever peed in the gutter. He even washed his hands with soap after using the toilet—he was a strange boy! The end of every school day, his parents were always inside the schoolyard waiting for him, and then, hand in hand, they would walk him to their fancy car. There were odd times when I ran and shouted him back for more play, but his parents would grab him by the hand and hurry away. It was great playing out with Robert, but he could be so loud and talked all the time, which hurt my ears and overpowered me. I would get a strange, sickly kind of pain, but not like the pain I felt when falling and bashing my knee. It wasn't an ordinary, everyday pain, the sort when Mum would give me a big, make-it-better kiss. I wanted to yell, 'Stop shouting and go away!' Instead, my lips snapped shut, and all the words, the letters, the full stops, and God knows what else, just bumped into each other and reversed down into a sickly lump at the bottom of my belly.

Mrs. Gregory's Year Three class is where all the maths books pulled everyone's heads down to maybe just a few inches above the pages. I was the exception. While all the other kids were working hard on adding up and taking away, I'd try copying their work, but they always wrapped their arms around their books to stop me from seeing. I really tried my best to understand why none of the numbers were happening for me. Okay, a few of them did light up, but that was about as close as me and numbers ever came.

Whenever the teacher started to teach, a big hole in the back of my head would open up, and everything being taught would enter and then trickle down between my shoulder blades, ending up on the floor in little mountains of learnings. I tried and tried to plug that hole—by going to bed early, eating more fish. Nothing worked. I thought joining the school library, as well as the local library, would help, but I soon found that the pictures were the best a book could do for me. I chose books on every subject the world had ever known, but it didn't change a thing: in fact, it made it worse. Some of the words in those books did try their very best by becoming larger, with some pages only having a few words, but none of it was working for me.

Me and books didn't give up on each other, though— quite the opposite. Those pictures and I would spend hours admiring each other. I wasn't like all the other kids, who would sit together and talk to each other about the adventures they were reading. I dreamed about taking part in what was happening in the pages. I was there in the book, driving and waving from the lead tank, liberating Paris.

One day, in class, while the other kids were hard at maths, I was playing with a green crayon found in my blazer pocket when that same crayon got stuck up my nose. I tried with my best nose-picking finger to get it out, but it was well and truly stuck. That's when Christine Brookes, the girl sat nearest to me, after seeing what had happened, started laughing, and the rest of the class joined in.

Mrs. Gregory told me to blow my nose harder than I had ever done before. There was more laughter when a dollop of snot and crayon shot into my hand, and I had to walk the entire aisle to make for the toilets, all because of Brookes. The teasing lasted almost two days. Robert was the only one who hadn't laughed.

Teacher always believed Christine Brookes, but that same morning, she caught her whispering across the aisle to her friend, Theresa. She stomped from her desk and slapped Christine so hard across the face that she knocked her glasses to the floor and broke them. My punishment for my face-pulling was six slaps with the ruler on the back of my bare legs. Mild, compared to what had happened to Christine.

Teacher would always ask the class to give Simpson a big clap because she never spilt a drop of ink. The following day, during morning break, I sneaked into the classroom and filled as many inkwells as I could with Mum's Andrews Liver Salts. As Miss Goody Two-Shoes Inkwell Filler started her job, pulling her nose up at everyone in the process, my prank began to bubble all over the desk. Miss Goody Two-Shoes wasn't told off. "Street," shouted Teacher, hands on hips. "Go stand in the wastebasket until the end of the lesson!"

I don't know why me and ink never made the best of friends. We tried so many times, but it just wouldn't happen. It helped the *ink*, though, which somehow ended up all over my clothes, books, and even my mouth.

Before Mr. Greenough, our headmaster, gave me three of his 'very best' for that ink, Robert sneaked over and gave me a candle, telling me to rub it on my hands. "The cane will slide off and won't hurt you the same". Candle wax or not, it still bloody hurt. Miss Goody Two-Shoes walked past to check if I was crying. I didn't give her the satisfaction of seeing me hurt, and so she resorted to shedding her crocodile tears.

Mum was called in around once a month, when the headmaster would threaten to send me to another school, one with a reputation for taking in slow or bad kids. Mum freaked, insisting she would make sure there would be improvement. To help, she bought me 'Robinson Crusoe', which was leant against a Bible on the front room shelf— home to the only two books in the house, which had never been read.

Kitty's Diary

Seven years old, Peter can't dress himself. Putting on all his clothes back to front and inside out.

It was Dad who paid for private maths lessons, but the teacher there gave up on me after just three sessions, saying I was lazy and not concentrating. I tried telling the teacher I really, *really* wanted to learn, but it just wouldn't happen for me. Counting up to fifty wasn't too bad, but it all started to go wrong once division and multiplication kicked in.

I couldn't understand how the other kids and maths had become the best of friends. While all the other kids' numbers were jumping and moving over, even standing on top of each other, numbers for me just wouldn't move. Some of their numbers were made to stand on the edge of the page until needed, and some numbers were taken away, never to be seen again. I could make up a number in my mind—any number—but the numbers stayed in the same spot, laying there in my head with no life in them. For me, there would never be any life in any of my numbers. Even when I nudged and shook the page to see if they would move and add up or take away, they never did. Whenever me and numbers really tried to get it together, everything else in my life just seemed to fall apart. I wasn't like the other kids. I wanted to be a little like them, but never managed it: numbers put paid to that.

Kitty's Diary

Peter came home crying. Teacher hit his head with the board duster.

Robert was the only kid I could talk with and relate to, but not in the washroom. Maybe it had something to do with the other kids in there throwing dirt at the big, scary **Now Wash Your Hands** poster. Robert, who was always clean as clean could be, would wash his hands twice. The pilot's helmet covering my ears helped a little, but I could still feel the boys bashing my ears as they shouted 'Backward!' over and

36

over. Once the tears were flowing, they would gather round, push and poke, laughing while dragging my helmet off and pulling my ears. I would escape to the place everyone hated: the boys' outside toilet with its open drains, used only in case of emergency or when the inside toilet was out of order.

The walls of that toilet, holding up fifty or sixty years of urine, were my safe haven. Alone, I would sit on the toilet bowl, where the stink never hit me. Those toilets and I became the best of friends, lasting all six years I was in junior school.

Home

Kitty's Diary
Rice all over the table. He has trouble filling the cup.

Dad's yellow bedroom and I were never given the chance at becoming friends. But me and my best snooping found Dad's 'secret box', which he thought was safe underneath his fireside chair. The bedroom key wasn't in there, though. The next best thing was the key to the 'best room'. Once inside the room, used only for special occasions, I would lock the door behind me and press my ear against the door to listen for his size nines. In the all clear, I would trampoline across the three-piece suite back and forth, again and again, over the shark-infested waters.

My other play area was the coal shed attached to the house in the back yard. It was almost twice the size of our kitchen. A long, iron chain dangled from a bolt fastened to the dust-covered coal shed wall. Inside, on an oil-stained bench, jumbled letters from a John Bull printing set, left behind by someone else struggling to say something. I always wanted to know who the stuff had belonged to, but there were never answers to any of my questions.

Me and John Bull soon became the best of friends. We spent hours together in that coal shed, making up bizarre words, our own silly words which didn't make any sense, but were fun to think up. All was well with Johnny and me. We were getting on like a house on fire until Dad came in one day. Looking at the very strange words, he sighed, and just said, "Never mind." Mum shouted me in for tea as Dad closed the coal shed door. I must have had a bad influence on John Bull because we didn't see each other again for some time.

It was later that evening I went to call for Clifford, a neighbour who would sometimes invite me in, and we would play in his kitchen or hang out in the back street, sat on the ground with our backs to the wall. Everything was great until his mum started shouting out into the back yard, "This can't go on. He keeps knocking on our door. Is there something wrong with him?"

Kitty's Diary

Peter thinks everyone wants to play ALL the time. One minute, he wants a friend. Next, he doesn't. He says he can't help it. It's like an 'ache'.

That night, restless and unable to sleep, my hands and my bedroom wall suddenly started playing shadows with the help of a few dogs, birds, and half a dozen rabbits, until I couldn't take my eyes off a huge eagle gliding up and back down the wall which somehow finally sent me off.

Early next morning, I walked to the cotton mill. Opening the sliding door into Dad's place of work, the stench of sulphur smacked my nose and my eyes tried to blink away the lines of dead dogs and cats: some with their heads off, some squashed, some with bullet wounds. Dad was in the fire-hole stoking the furnaces. He said something about two shillings for every dead cat and dog that the police brought in. My feet and mouth were welded to the steel floor. My thoughts were nothing I could explain. Dad clanged open the incinerator door and turned to pick up the rover and tabby he had somehow kept separate from the coal and oil. Then, with a clean cloth, he wiped off the dirt and blood and gave them a last stroke before throwing them in. He left the door open as I stepped forward and watched someone's pet melt into nothing.

Kitty's Diary

Letter from June. Usual gossip. So WHAT if Mr. Jones'
boiled ham is not as good as it was, and who cares if he
doesn't get his eggs from Ronnie Smith anymore?!

4

LOCKED DOORS

Kitty's Diary

October 1954

He's mad—only fruit and veg from across the road that we don't need to pay money for.

Dad was heading down to the cellar, when, for some reason, he stopped on the stairs and, for just a second, I saw the shadow of someone down there, but who? How? The cellar was in the middle of the house and that was the only way in. Dad turned back, glanced at me, then quickly shut and locked the cellar door behind him. Every time I asked, he said there was no one there, and that it was my 'imagination'. Regardless, I *did* see someone.

It was another door hiding secrets. Whenever he was out,

I knocked on it and shouted as loud as I could, but there was never any answer. Or I would chance my luck and try the handle of the mysterious yellow bedroom door. I even peeped through the keyhole, but there was never anything to be seen. I couldn't help returning to that same yellow door, hoping that on one of those rare days he was late and rushing for work, he would leave it unlocked. Whenever I asked about his bedroom, it was always, "Nothing in there for *you*."

There were times he would hurry back to double-check the door. Every couple of months, he would rub a damp cloth over the yellow door's handle, as if he was wiping it clean of fingerprints.

Breakfast was made up of various fruits and nuts. I could choose whatever I wanted from the shop across the road. Dad would later ask the fruit and veg owner if I had minded my Ps and Qs. "Always," always came the answer.

I was the first in our street to eat a banana after wartime rations, while the other kids, if they were lucky, got toast and jam and maybe a special treat of cornflakes before church on a Sunday.

On most rainy days, I would play ball with the stairs, aiming the ball up at my bedroom door which would, in turn, bounce it back down into my arms before I'd kick it back up. Odd times, the door would knock the ball sideways and bring to life the dark landing which usually refused to join in. Once the stairs got bored of me, I would chop wooden bobbins near the back kitchen ready for the front room fire. Other days, it was marbles on the carpet floor.

School

Rainy school days would run everyone up through the Boys' entrance and into the hall where we would stand in lines, nose touching the back of someone's head. Like cut-out figures waiting to be stretched, soaked to the skin and steaming next to the old radiators. Whenever we were in the hall, I couldn't take my eyes off the picture on the wall a few feet up above my head. Encased in a glass frame, a photograph of the first eleven holding the winner's cup. Clean, Brylcreemed hair, perfectly straight and parted as though split with an axe. They wore a pre-war strip and bullnose boots. I was so jealous of the ball at the proud-looking Captain's feet. Every part of me wanted to be in that picture. Even yards away from it, I could almost smell the dubbin leather casey ball, and ached to take it home. I needed to know how to win a place in a team like that. Me in the middle, different to all the others in their white shirts. Me standing alone, even though I would be in top-middle position. Important. The last one: GOALKEEPER.

They called me crazy.

Fearlessly wearing the dark-coloured goalkeeping jersey, I promised myself that's who I was going to be. Different. Nine years old and *certain* I was going to be a famous goalkeeper.

Break times, the school grounds teacher would come bashing my ears with questions about me sitting by myself on the floor. The more she screamed, the more I wanted to sit there and be alone, wet or not. Playtime was a massive beast hurrying from one side of the schoolyard to the other, monstering round and round, side to side, with its forty pairs of legs. What I imagined it was like being in the middle of a tornado.

I needed the other side of the school yard, away from it all, when, "Street," shouted the teacher, "go see if the other boys will let you play with them." Then it was my usual escape trick, with my legs aiming for the outside toilet and its urine-stained walls, always there to welcome me and my moans, tears, or laughter.

Sometimes, instead of tag with the other boys in the playground, which wasn't me, I'd play two-ball with Pauline and Theresa. I thought it would somehow help me improve my concentration, and they were glad to teach me to play alongside them. I even tried standing on my hands as they did, with their skirts tucked up into their knickers, and they would laugh when I lost balance and fell down. My eyes, hands, and the wall, for whatever reason, didn't get it together, but the girls and I did manage to share a skipping rope with the street's lamp post. I was fine with just the two girls but any more would have forced a tightening in my chest. I'd have the feeling of being overtaken, causing more stress, and then confusing smells, not obvious to others, would climb up into my nose. I would confide in them how my nose was different from theirs. How sometimes I would wake smelling custard, even though there was none. There were other regular smells too, like kippers, or worse still, when I was feeling sad, diesel or petrol. When the boys found out, that was it.

My so-called 'jokes' came back to hit me, so I stopped telling everyone about invisible smells, and there was *no way* I could ever tell them about me and the wall.

Once home, after finding my ball in the coal shed, I picked it up and threw it to the toilet wall at the bottom of my yard. It passed it straight back. The excitement of the ball running toward me and then up into my arms was wonderful, immediate. This was me and how I would follow in my hero goalkeeper Eddie Hopkinson's footsteps. I had seen pictures of him in The Buff—Bolton's Saturday evening sports paper. Me and that wall, for those few hours, became the best of friends.

It was in that backyard, over the next few weeks, where

me and my ball came to life with the help of the red brick wall and a ten-foot-wide box which was something to do with the electric or gas board—perfect, being the same height and width of a football goal. Where me, the wall, and ball would become the awesome three. Warm-up was just gently side-footing the ball to the wall, who always passed back to me. Okay, at times it would be passed halfway down the street, but I'd quickly chase after it and slam it back to the wall.

Others had friendships, some closer than others. I had two major friends: ball and the wall. The three of us were inseparable. That night, I took it all out—everything about school and other kids wanting to hurt me for reasons I didn't understand—slamming the ball hard against the wall. It headed for the right-hand corner: wall dived upward and slammed the ball back right, making me run as it bounced and bobbed over the cobbled street. Without hesitation, I picked it up and threw it back to the wall. Not just any old throw—precise, to the player up the field.

My job that evening was to paint a circle on the wall just a little bigger than the width of a football.

5

ROBERT

My dream wish was for Mum to take just one hour off work and come into school to bend the headteacher's ear, but she could never get time off. I didn't understand how the other kids' parents, who were probably on the same shift work, could take time out and come to the playground and into school to check everything was all right with their child. Maybe it was something to do with the time they made her wait in the corridor, as kids, teachers, and God knows who else passed her by. She had only wanted to ask the teacher to stop calling me stupid. In class, I used to wish a large hole would also open in the other kids' heads, as it did with me, and all that learning dribble out the back of *their* heads. My wish never came true. It would have been great to hear other mums and dads shouting, 'Our Michael's not backward' or

'Our Pauline's not silly'. Sometimes I was grateful for being called 'backward', but parents and kids didn't want to know me. The kids would laugh and tell their mums and dads about me, who would, in turn, talk to the teachers. Once, out of school, one of the mums had asked some other mothers if there was something wrong with me.

The playground teachers never asked *why* I preferred sitting alone on the pavement. They never asked *why* I always cried and sobbed when other boys would grab and pull off my leather pilot's helmet, before holding me down and shouting into my ears. Crying still didn't bring over the teachers. Some days were bad; sometimes they were far worse. My friend, the outside toilet, was my escape. Where I didn't mind sitting next to the piss of the floor's open gutter. It was my quiet place, and toilet and I became used to each other's company.

All the boys, including me and Robert, were called into the hall after someone had daubed dog shit on some posters. No one had admitted to it, which, somehow, made the teachers more determined to find out who had done it, but they never did. At least, that's what we were told, but it never happened again. Even now, all these years later, I don't know why but I always had the feeling Robert had daubed those posters. Despite that, while he often talked about getting dirty, he was frightened to, and always looked at me with jealous eyes. At least, that's how it seemed.

Robert came into his own with bird watching, learning their names and the kind of whistle he could attract them with. He always had twice as much bread as I did, and he'd share so that we ended up with the same amount to throw to the birds.

He was the only one who didn't laugh when Mr. Horrocks walloped me on the side of my head with the board duster. His arm shot up, asking Teacher why I had been made to stand in the wastebasket. "Because he acts the fool. We all know he's clever, but he *will* insist on not using full stops or capital letters."

They were things everyone else understood but were not happening for me; even Robert tried to explain to the teacher. For some reason, my brain just didn't get it. There were times I found it impossible to sleep for wondering why. And, odd times, Mum would run into my bedroom after hearing me shout for Robert. Often, I would cry myself to sleep, holding onto my teddy, thinking about the time he did a crazy dance after I had shown him how to light a fire with just two matches and no paper.

Kitty's Diary

October 1957

Peter's spending more time on his own playing marbles in the outside toilet.

Morning school milk breaks, Robert and I would sneak to the back of the classroom, where Teacher couldn't see us, drinking our milk and swapping butties. It was our dare, sneaking those few minutes, each time trying for a few more. I think he was more excited than I was.

When Robert wasn't in school, he'd be off somewhere fancy, like on his parents' boat sailing around the coast. It was those times I preferred being on my own, because, for whatever reason, the other kids would do their very best to overpower or tease me. I didn't know why, but that was the way of it. It's probably why I wanted to stand on my own, in my own space, in the playground. But the teacher would always grab me by my shoulders and march me to the middle of the playground to join in the other kids' games. My head would begin to squeeze in on itself and I would want to vomit, but, instead, I'd freeze there as the other kids just played around me. After that, the teachers would give up and hurry me back into school.

Kitty's Diary

Mrs. Porrits complained about Peter always waiting on their doorstep, early mornings after I've left for work.

One time, Robert's parents dropped him off at our house. Mum had beckoned them in for a cup of tea and a slice of her homemade lemon drizzle cake; they refused. In my bedroom,

Robert wore a gas mask while we played war games. He was protecting my fort with his red and black lead soldiers, who began flying and shooting down enemy planes, which somehow made him laugh. He whipped off the mask, crying happy tears, when, without warning, creaking floorboards brought Mum crashing into our battlefield to ask Robert how long he could stay and would his parents be returning to collect him.

After cake and pop, I suggested digging for pretend pirate treasure in our back garden. I told Robert he could use my clothes so he could keep his own clean. It was the first time I saw him go back into himself, squirming. He was a different, more anxious Robert than the one I'd just been playing soldiers with. Without lifting his head, he refused. Our mood changed down a couple of gears when we left behind that part of the garden to sit on the back step, waiting for something to happen. It was there that he confessed, *wished*, he had as much fun as I did. It wasn't long before Mum came out to say, "Robert, your car is here."

In the school playground the next day, I told Robert about me digging for pirate treasure in the back garden. How, when lifting big clods of mud, the top button of my pants had flown off. Robert laughed until his sides ached. He apologised for laughing.

Home from school, I walked into the front room and in the far corner was a large television which hadn't been there that morning. I cried happy tears and, in my excitement, ran to switch it on, but then decided instead to wait for Dad. On the table beside it was a small box. I read the label out loud, 'Airfix Model Spitfire'—a model aeroplane waiting there for us to engineer together.

Kitty's Diary

He can't do Airfix models. Glue everywhere—even in his mouth!

The smell of glue reminded my nose of paint or nail varnish remover. Dad laughed when I told him about the big yellow button, and how it had been the first button Mum had picked out of her button box. There was never any rummaging through the dozens and dozens of buttons in her brightly-coloured tin box. It was always just the very first one found, the one that she used. The bright yellow button was double the size needed for those short pants, and she had even cut the buttonhole to fit. It glowed like a beacon over my belly. Of course, everyone at school laughed, though it seemed odd that everyone should find a large yellow button so silly. "It's all right. No one else can see it," Mum would say.

But the *whole world* could see the huge button, boasting its very best yellow.

I found an empty Bird's Custard Powder tin which had

been retired to the pantry, and then went to empty her button box onto the table. Buttons of every size and colour were bouncing all over the place. I picked out all the buttons matching the size and colour of my pants and jackets, and placed them back into Mum's tin. The Bird's Custard Powder tin, with the all the weird, oversized buttons, went under my bed to be sure I would never be laughed at again. Relaxed, I shared the rest of the afternoon with the BBC's *Bill and Ben the Flowerpot Men*.

Mum did her best teaching me to sew and cook, but time and energy were the main reasons she couldn't help with school or anything else due to all the washing on a Friday night, ready for the Saturday wash when the room would be turned into a Turkish bath, with all the steam rising from the dolly tub. Seeing her from the kitchen, humped over the washboard, she always somehow looked as though she was cut in two. Grabbing at the shoulders of Dad's shirt and pushing it down until its back would arch and bubble up. She would watch it, then thump, lift and slop it into another tub in the corner, which would hold it until Mum was ready to put it through the wringer. Then I would help turn the handle to squeeze out the excess water. It was the most hated job in the house, along with taking up the six-by-four front room rug. We had to drag it out and then lift it onto the washing line to beat out all the dirt, fag ash, and God knows what else.

It was on one weekend, when the carpet had to be dragged out, when two men, complete strangers to us, burst through the back gate without warning and made for the kitchen, struggling with something heavy.

"Who the hell are *you*?" Mum shouted.

Right there, in the centre of the kitchen, stood an almost brand-new Empress Washing Machine, together with its instruction leaflet. "He wants his drains doing again, tell Thomas Edgar," the taller of the two informed her. Nothing more was said.

Two weeks later, a third man came in with an almost brand-new Hoover. Again, nothing else was said. He disappeared as quickly as he came. Mum cried with joy. We had an idea they were from Dad's 'hush-hush friends'. He never said where or how we came about those costly items. When asked, it was a shrug of the shoulders. Mum knew for certain no money was ever handed over.

Mum and I started baking bread and pies together. There were no scales in the house, so Mum had to teach me using cups and spoons, and a pinch of this and that. It came so naturally to me. So simple, as though baking, for me, was a gift. It would be my next career, once my football one was over.

A few weeks later, Robert kept asking about coming to our house to start digging for treasure. Great! We planned everything, just like before. He would wear some of my old clothes and, when we were done playing, he would change back into his own. That was the plan, but then Mum decided we would be going out instead.

Ten minutes walked us up to Astley Bridge playground where we reminisced about the time when mud and smiles were all over us. We had been relaxing for about an hour when we heard Mum calling us back, having seen Robert's parents' big posh car drive round.

Mum hurried him to the sink and wiped him clean of everything, including his broad smile. Spotless, with his hair parted to the left, as though cut with an axe, he hurried out to the kerb and got into the big car.

Neither his mum nor dad waved.

After school, Robert and I started meeting up on Astley Bridge Park, where he always tried swinging the monkey bars, but never made it across. Tired of the swings, we would talk about wild birds, like the shrikes, blue tits, or the clever magpies who visited the park. Later, we would hit the merry-go-round before heading over to the big slide, which we rubbed with Warburton's greaseproof bread wrappers and, from the railings, would watch the kids go flying off the end, and laugh as they landed in a puddle of water at the bottom.

Back in school, Robert was the only one not to laugh when Teacher walloped me over the head with the duster, because it would 'knock some sense into me' for being too lazy to learn 'simple' sums. "Look around you, Street. Everyone else is doing their work. Why don't you join them, instead of just sitting there twiddling your thumbs?"

I was rubbing the side of my head, feeling sick, when he finally said, "Street, go and stand in the corner until you stop crying."

That was the weekend I tried teaching Robert how to kick a football. His timing was so far out that he gave up trying. He started crying and, without saying a word, left for home.

In school on Monday, he never said anything about his tears.

One Sunday, when Robert and I were in the park, he lost his grip on the monkey bars because some bright spark had greased them with Vaseline. Yes, the fall shook him up, because it was the first time he had ever fallen from anything. The cotton wool he had been wrapped in made sure of that. But after, sitting on the park bench, he somehow felt proud of himself.

When his parents came to the park looking for him, Robert quickly dropped his feet from the bench when we saw his mum come steaming toward us. The look she gave shook me so much. It was as though she wanted to harm me. She grabbed hold of Robert and dragged him off, and, when they reached the top of the park, he turned and waved, but his mum didn't give me time to wave back.

I was back to training with my wall.

That was the summer of finding me and who I was. The realisation I was different from all the other kids. Alone, but never lonely. I found it hard to comprehend why some of the other kids cried about being lonely. To me, lonely was a kind of freedom for my ears and my whole body, giving the *real* me a rest. I realised I was special, because I was different from all the other kids, and I think they knew I was different as I would spend hours playing football with a red brick wall, and sometimes with the lamp post who treated us to some light when me and the wall got it together late nights. Otherwise, it would just stand there, enjoying the game, maybe considering himself a reserve if ever the wall should need a rest.

Mum's every-so-often friends

Mum's only friend, Abrahana, and her daughter, Rachel, would often visit us out of the blue. There was never any letter or note. They would turn up, never explaining where they had been or what they had been doing.

It had been almost a year since they last came. I always thought Mum must have known where they had been and where they vanished off to after their short visits. As always, it was secrets and more secrets. They would stay a weekend and then leave again without saying a word or even goodbye.

Regardless of the many times I asked, Mum never told me why they had to go or where they were going in such a hurry. She always dodged my questions about when their next visit would be, or even how she had come to know them.

I also didn't understand why Dad didn't seem pleased when Rachel and I played together. For those few hours, she was like a big sister to me. She never raised her voice, and I didn't mind her sitting on the chair in my bedroom, practising her make-up skills on me and rouging my cheeks. In return, I would plait her hair, and then, with her new plaits, she would wet the comb and redesign mine. Meanwhile, Mum would be chatting for hours with Abrahana. But the following morning, they would be gone again with no note, no goodbye, nothing. I would return to goalkeeper training with my wall, who would still be there, regardless of the many times I might leave it to be with others, or for a day out with Mum.

Bonfire

In the autumn of '57, Robert and I sneaked in more playtime, with secret notes and symbols on the stone flags or walls of the schoolyard, and the plan for a bonfire was born. Dad had shown me how to light a fire with just two matches and no paper. Robert didn't believe it could be done. I don't know why, but he just suddenly started jumping up and down, dancing around me. The more I laughed, the more he danced, only stopping to take a breath. He begged me to show him this new world-beating trick which would change everything. It was as though we had just invented something the world had never known.

He flopped to the ground as I promised Dad would be there to make sure it all went to plan, and it was there, on that school floor, we both agreed that this bonfire night was going to be the best the world had ever seen. He started dancing again and we laughed until our sides hurt, crashing us to the ground where I said he hadn't to tell anyone—it was our secret. He promised and crossed his heart. There was a short silence before he started talking about bringing firelighters, extra matches, and a torch in case it was raining.

Dad helped us collect the wood from Wolfenden Street Timber Yard. We promised him we would stand well back as he started the fire. We had planned everything, including buckets of water to keep on guard in case the wooden fence caught alight. Everything was in place: nothing could go wrong.

Saturday morning, I was up early, too excited to have breakfast, and ready with some old clothes for Robert to wear.

I waited and waited. It was getting dark. I ate my meal in the outside toilet, crying, wondering what had gone wrong.

He promised he would be down and we would eat black peas and share some of Mum's homemade parkin cake.

By nine-thirty, I knew he wasn't coming.

Neither Robert nor I had known his parents had other plans. They'd never said a word.

After that, I couldn't understand why they stopped him from coming round. It was only later that I found out they'd gone down to Anglesey, North Wales, to try out their new boat, and that something had gone wrong. The entire family were thrown into the water and Robert and his sister, the only ones who couldn't swim, had both drowned.

At school, everyone was led into the school hall to be told of the accident. All our exciting plans had been our very last. I would never again make friends with anyone whose parents had big fancy cars. Everyone in the school was asked to sign a card for Robert's parents, telling them how sorry we were. Every morning of November 5th, even now all these years later, I can't help thinking—if only he'd come down with me for our bonfire.

6

ST. JUDE'S R. C. JUNIOR SCHOOL

Gemma Smyth

Whenever Mum left for the cotton mill, silence would bang every inch of our house. Bored and alone, I would crash into Dad's front room chair and dangle my legs over the arms, twirling them over the reflections from the summer window on the carpet. Just like Dad, I would hold onto the frayed edge to lift myself from the chair.

Ready to go out, I would leave my ball in the comfort of the chair, then aim my legs for school and its warm cellar, smelling of coal, where the caretaker, Mr. Crompton, always made me a cup of tea and talked Bolton Wanderers, Eddie Hopkinson, and the weekend's result.

My school, St. Jude's, was organising the football House

teams. 'Cardinal Newman' was the name of my house. Our first match was the beginning of who I was and who I was going to be. The teacher congratulated me on such a great game. I was, from then on, the regular junior school goalkeeper. I thought life at school, and the name-calling, was going to cool off once I had been picked for the house team. I was wrong. Jealousies were fired louder and clearer into my ears, mostly by Michael Bull, a blonde-haired boy who always had turned-up toes in the shining shoes his father made him polish every morning before breakfast. His parents bought him a new fountain pen almost every week to give his handwriting a better chance of improvement. It didn't. He was good in goal, but not as good as me. And whatever he did, he was always late, convincing the teacher that some other kid had caused him to be late. Whatever wrong he did, he never got caught, blamed, or punished. Even the times he would wait by the girls' toilet, then run in, banging on the doors. He seemed to get a kick from hearing them scream. Yes, the teacher once told him not to do it again, but he did, and yet nothing else was ever said to him again. I think the teachers were scared of his older brother coming back: a brother who had been at the school three years before and had a reputation for fighting, even with the police.

Gemma Smyth (with the red pigtails and three older brothers), seeing Michael go into the boys, ran in as he was peeing and pushed him. His face hit the urine-stained wall, forcing him to pee himself before running out. Her brothers, who had reputations, warned him not to grass on their sister. It stopped his pranks.

Secrets

Alone, but never lonely, I took two eggs from the kitchen back to my bedroom. I smashed them on my head and started redesigning my hair, spiking it first, then flattening it. My hard-set hair looked as though it had been painted black and plastered down. Windproof and unmovable.

My bedroom mirror couldn't stop laughing. It shook up and down and started to pull a face as though it was about to vomit. Within the hour, I had washed it out and went to share a few hours with my outside toilet playing marbles, and later, even though I knew there wouldn't be any treasure, I started digging in the back yard. I was almost knee-deep when my small border spade crunched into a skeleton. I screamed for Dad, who came running out with Mum. I told them I had found a body. I always knew there wasn't pirate stuff, but there was nothing else to do and it seemed a good idea to keep going, but I often dug a foot or so just in case. Even though I knew nothing was there, I kept on digging. I promised myself: if I did find hidden treasure, it would pay for us to holiday at Blackpool for a lifetime.

They looked down into my dig when Dad said, "That's Rex, the big German Shepherd." He paused and, instead of telling me about the dog, picked up my ball and ran us into the back street where he slammed it into the wall for me to chase. We shared half an hour's kickabout, but no more clues were given about the skeleton in the back yard. The third time I asked him, he left me for his comfy chair, Woodbines, and tea with seven sugars. I followed him into the kitchen when I noticed he was crying. Mum said he'd got something in his eye, but I knew different because his face was twisted up and tears were flooding. He walked out and went back down into his secret hideaway where all the monsters lived.

Kitty's Diary

Peter came home crying. Teacher made him stand in the corner all lesson because he couldn't cover his book with the newspaper. He couldn't fold it the right way, or even understand why he should.

I'll swing for that school one of these days.

Eddie Hopkinson

I asked Mum again about his hideaway and how it was that the monsters in the shadows didn't get him. She just smiled and gently rubbed my back. I loved her doing that; it often sent me to sleep. My eyes would always close and I would go into my own world, picturing myself standing on the goal line next to Eddie Hopkinson. He would be teaching me how to dive, this way and that. Me following every word and action. He let me wear his famous cap, and with each dive he demonstrated, I followed. I never once felt any pain after landing from those high dives to catch the ball. We would stand beside each other on his goal line before walking together to mark his goal area. He would scrape the right side while I did the same on the left. Shaking hands, he told me that one day soon I would be on his goal line. "That's my *dream*," I'd call out when Mum finally shook me awake.

My part-time friend, Clifford, who lived next door, would meet me in the street, ready to knock about. Everything was great until his mum came to our house one day, shouting, "Peter has to stop waiting for Clifford on our doorstep early mornings!" There was a short silence before, "It's every day, this can't go on. Is there something wrong with him? Does he not understand that people need their privacy?"

Kitty's Diary

Peter went mad, screaming and beating himself when he got told to stop waiting on Clifford's doorstep. Says he can't help it.

Me and the bedroom wall would play shadows with a few dogs, birds, and rabbits. The animal shapes would go away when I pulled a chair over to the bedroom window to count all the people going in and out of the shops. It could be all day, even all weekend, watching them and trying to guess where they'd been or where they were going. I would sometimes let George, my teddy bear, sit next to me to watch all the comings and goings of Blackburn Road.

7

UNCLE DAVID (*who wasn't my real uncle*)

Christmas 1957 was one of the best so far. Everything was set with a Christmas cake and a turkey feeling sorry for itself on the table. Two pirates were sitting opposite me, one with a black eyepatch over his thick-rimmed glasses and a red handkerchief over his head. Mum, the other pirate, had a white handkerchief over her red hair and wore a thin moustache like Errol Flynn's. I was the only one in Christmas clothes. I couldn't stop laughing, and Vick, trying to shake the pirate patch off his head, couldn't stop barking.

It was then when Mum and Dad introduced me to 'Magic Robot'. George, with his one eye dangling down, wasn't best pleased. He thought Magic Robot was a bit of a smart-arse. But no matter how much of a bad day that robot was having, it never ever gave the wrong answer. George and I,

'The Magical Amazing Robot' board game.

instead of turning it the three times on that circular mirror—as per the board game's instructions, would turn and turn it until we were dizzy. Each time it spun round, we would sit back praying it would point to the wrong answer. I would sit George on my knee and fold his arms across his chest, ready for those belly laughs at seeing the robot fall over, or, better still, point that stick of his to the wrong answer. No. It never fell over, not even once. Not even a funny wobble. He would stand upright. Back straight, pointing that silly little stick to the correct answer. In the end we gave up trying to catch him out and welcomed him in the correct and proper way into our house. Okay, he wasn't good at marbles or football, and he was rubbish at dominoes, but, my God, he knew his general knowledge. In fact, he was more than clever: he was magic. He was *my* Magic Robot.

There was no waiting for Mum or Dad to open the front door. It was Uncle David's usual one knock followed by his two extra loud knocks and then three lighter ones before his trench coat, inches from the ground, and lapels crammed with pin badges would walk him into our front room. His hair and beard were not that long, but his stink told me there had been no baths for at least a month. Mum said he stayed in different homes while roaming the country, doing odd jobs for a crust or a bar of soap for his razor. He traipsed up and down the North West with others like him, too traumatised from his war experiences to be part of family life again.

In his excitement, he would always shout, "Happy birthday, Peter!"

"I keep telling you," Dad would say, "Peter's birthday is Christmas Day."

There would be a long silence; then, "Well, now it's his birthday today too! Happy birthday, Peter."

His birthday presents and wishes never came on the same day. His gift that late summer was a bottle top from a Magee Marshalls Indian Pale Ale. He flicked the cork from the bottle top and pressed the top into my shirt: "Hey presto, your badge of honour!"

Uncle David stood to attention and saluted me, and I did the same back to him. Then he handed me his highly prized de Havilland badge from his lapel: the very one he had always talked about. It reminded him of his time there as an aero engineer.

He was ready to leave when he hesitated, as though he'd forgotten something, and picked a piece of coal from the bucket by the fire. Turning it in his hand, he located the seam and split it with the poker repeatedly until there were several smaller pieces of coal, no bigger than a postage stamp. Dad smiled and nodded. I hadn't a clue what was going on.

He threw all but three of the pieces back in the bucket.

"Do us a favour, Peter? Go and rinse these three pieces under the tap."

I looked at Dad. Dad nodded. I rinsed them and put them

back into Uncle David's hand, where he patted them dry before handing one of the postage stamp-sized pieces of coal to Dad. He put it into his mouth and gave a sigh of relief as he leaned back in his chair then started sucking on it. Uncle Peter nodded in a way that suggested it was my turn to taste the coal.

Strange how the pair of them just watched, waiting for me to put that piece of coal into my mouth and suck on it. I wanted Mum to walk in. She didn't. I wanted Vick to bark. He didn't. I wanted something to happen. It didn't. So I tasted the black. I pulled a face, waiting for the black to kick in. It didn't. There was just the slight taste of sulphur. They both laughed. I went to check my tongue in the mirror: there was no black.

"Do you good," Dad said. "Best thing for your stomach."

"There's nothing wrong with my stomach!"

"You need to know these things," Dad said.

"You should always know about these things," agreed Uncle David, before pulling an array of other peculiar items from his pocket: a length of thick twine with knots about a foot apart—a measuring string, maybe; some curly bits of bark—thin as paper; a pencil with both ends sharpened; a penknife; and a petrol lighter fitted into a rifle cartridge. Then he put them all back in his pocket. I wanted to know everything there was to know about his bits and bats (and wished I could have them), but he didn't say a word about any of them; except for the string, which he used for measuring on his gentry estate jobs, like 'puddling' flowers to stop them drying out. Uncle David laughed, rubbing a hand over his bald head.

Mum and I left, leaving them to their games and chat, to go shopping. Blackburn Road walked us down to the butcher's, round the other side of Iron Church, where Mum bought lots of sausages.

"How's Tommy?"

Mum smiled back, "Very well."

Mum would always say that Bolton town centre, with its market hall, was a kind of freedom. Among the bustling crowds, she would hold my hand tight in hers as she checked everything on sale with her other hand. Always into the knick-knack shops to finally buy, instead of barter or be asked how Tommy was. Bolton town centre was the place she could breathe again.

Before home, it was into Gregory and Porritts, with its chandelier sparkling over everyone, then prayers across the road in St. Patrick's, where we lit candles and I asked Jesus to help me be as good a goalkeeper as Eddie Hopkinson. Finally, it was vanilla ice cream in the Milk Bar on Bradshawgate.

At home, Dad was pulling out his bunch of keys, which he always kept in his boilersuit pocket. He and Uncle were standing in front of the cellar door: the very same door which held back those cold-breathing monsters. Dad blew out the dust from the keys. "Not for young boys," said Uncle David.

When the stone floor screeched open the cellar door, they stepped down into the darkness, suddenly both covered in yellow. They were halfway down when I caught a glimpse of a third man standing back in the dark. My terror hurried me into the front room to play marbles, well away from the monster down in the cellar.

It was an hour before they resurfaced, safe and sound. Finally, they sparked up Woodbines and swigged mugs of sweet tea. Then, before heading out into the cold, Uncle David wrapped a sheet of the Bolton Evening paper around his chest. He stuffed some more into his pockets, then fit a Woodbine behind his right ear. It was always his right.

There was no 'thank you' to Mum or Dad, just a nod and a 'goodbye' in his usual posh voice. That was it until his next visit. When—we never knew.

I returned to the back street and joined my friend, the red brick wall, still standing there waiting for me, eager for a game of footy. Diving this way and that, never forgetting to pass the ball back to me. Sometimes it was on the left wing, maybe the right, even down the centre: a great forward. Some days *it* would want to be goalkeeper.

***

Kitty's Diary

January 1958

Tony Potter is bullying Peter for no reason.

My Best Friend, the Toilet

Our school had been given the honour of showing our formation dancing skills to the town's new Mayor on prize-giving day. He had once been a pupil there. We had three weeks to get it perfect.

The teacher said we were to cross over to reach the other dancer, then hold the other person's hand and move around to a different person. To let go and then change to whoever.

It started and ended with, "Street, what in God's name are you doing?"

I stopped, confused. Standing there in the centre of everyone while the bottoms of my short pants had, for whatever reason, taken to twirling themselves round. The floorboards grabbed hold of my shoes, tight, and wouldn't let go.

Teacher's face exploded, sending her shrapnel all over me, especially my ears, and my face was burning. I didn't understand why it was just me who couldn't do it. They were all looking at me, and the music seemed to be getting so loud that it was banging my ears. I was ready to die. I made an excuse about needing the toilet.

Freedom again, with the outside toilet and I sharing more glorious moments away from all the noise. I tried to figure out the names and the various body parts scribbled across the grey lines of urine left from kids trying to aim highest up the pissing wall. And a new message: 'Kilroy was here'. Who was Kilroy, and what was he doing in *my* toilet space? I stayed there until I heard the bell.

That night in my bedroom, I dreamt I was a sheep. Just following, copying, not even thinking. Just like everyone else. Like enjoying those afternoon school dance classes instead of spending the afternoon in the outside toilet, where no one came looking. I was alone, but not lonely. I was there out of the way. Sometimes I would dream of being a sheep, so I could be like everyone else.

Our outside toilet, which Mum would traipse out to every morning with our night-time piss-pots before going to work, became redundant after a posh inside one ganged up with a nice blue basin and bath. They took over our spare bedroom, where my khaki fort and lead soldiers were stationed.

Only I used the bath. Mum never fully bathed. She would wipe down while never taking off any clothes. She didn't even take off her rosary. Strange, her ritual body wash and the way she would use a damp, soaped flannel under her layers of clothes. It would happen three, sometimes four, times a day. After each body wash, she would treat her red hair with a tablespoon of olive oil, backed up with Nivea or Pond's moisturiser cream. Rubbing her little finger over her red lipstick to rouge her cheeks. She would treat herself to one dab of her favourite perfume, 'Evening In Paris', then carry on with all her hard work.

My rainy day, outside toilet always looked bored, probably from doing nothing except sit there, while reading the strips of Bolton Evening News strung to the green wooden door. Meanwhile, the paraffin lamp that stood in the corner, surrounded by patched strands of whitewash, helped keep flies and God knows what else away.

It was my escape place, with the whiteness of it all lighting up the very best marble assault course—with its cracks, dips, and holes in those few stone flags—which most kids could only dream about. That outside toilet lifted me and my marbles to become and remain champions of Blackburn Road.

On rainy days, I would spend most of my time inside that outdoor toilet. It seemed to come alive with purpose whenever I turned up. Instead of just letting it sit there, twiddling its thumbs, waiting for company, I would go in and, together, we would spend the afternoon. I would play marbles as it looked over my shoulder. Okay, sometimes, especially in the hot summer months and light nights, it was bored. We both understood that, and how I would mostly be out in the park or back street playing footy. It must have been six months since that green wooden toilet door had stopped holding up strips of the Bolton Evening News and how, strangely, Dad would wedge it open like he knew it was keeping all the sun to itself. Okay, the door sometimes complained by suddenly screeching so loudly over the stone flagged floor that my ears closed down. That was the day me and that outside toilet found each other. It was the perfect place for marbles. I wanted my food in the outside toilet, too, but it was a big 'no'. I would've won a world record for the fastest time eating dinner. I had to get back to sharing my place with the toilet. We all became inseparable, with the paraffin storm lamp watching us from the corner. Its excuse for being there: to stop the pipes from freezing up. It was just a pity it couldn't take part. Instead, it would stand there, helping me rise through the neighbourhood marble league rankings from one of the worst marble players to one of the best.

8

RACHEL

Kitty's Diary

February 1958

Thomas is paying for Peter to have swimming lessons.
Two shillings, sixpence a week. He wants me to learn too.

My Best Friend, the Red Brick Wall

Months after his death, I was still seeing me and Robert in
Astley Bridge Park, and the time he'd tried swinging the
monkey bars. In his frustration, asking me to swing across
again so he could see if there was some kind of technique to
it all—there wasn't.

The back street of 339 Blackburn Road was *my* place,

where I would chalk garages on the ground and pretend to wind up lifts and crash my Matchbox cars into our outside toilet wall. That back street was the place where my dreams were born and played out. My mind would take me everywhere possible, and, sometimes, impossible. It's where I used to help Dan Dare beat the Mekons. It's where I would score the winning goal for Melchester Rovers after Roy had passed the ball back to me in that outside-right position while running up the wing. It's where I used to be the Bolton Wanderers' goalkeeper, and save every single shot aimed for the goal. It was *brilliant*. That back street was my childhood and that goal-sized wall never let me down or ran off with a new friend of mine. I never overpowered it and, in return, that wall never overpowered me. There it was, *my* wall, looking so cool standing there. Our training sessions would prepare me for whatever team I could trial for. To be chosen for a team, I had to get my position right. I had to be goalkeeper—I couldn't dribble and keep the ball at my feet like the other boys could.

I took in a breath and looked at the wall before tossing a coin. Heads, I won. The wall never sulked over losing a toss. I looked left and right, whistled, then hit the ball as hard as I could for the left-hand corner. It was the perfect pass. And a perfect goal when the wall dived left, saved and passed it back to me, maybe twenty yards in front, making me run and catch it before the street lamp tried to get in on the act.

Mind you, it probably wouldn't have, because it was happy just standing there watching. I trapped and kicked the ball over to my far right. Warm-up completed and breathless, I was ready to pick up the ball for my goalkeeper training with the wall when I heard, "Hi, Peter".

"Rachel!"

We hugged. It had been two years since Abrahana and Rachel last visited, turning up out of the blue, as usual. It was always a Sunday morning when they would appear, and we would go to mass together. I couldn't help but think, why Sunday? When I asked Mum later where they had been, again it was just, "None of our business".

The wall never sulked when Rachel appeared. We sat opposite, on the back step, listening to her mum's stories about this mystical place called Sweden. There were jaw-dropping moments, with tales of an Iron Age woodland, Hållet Skogen, where stones the size of a bus shelter would roll down hills, squashing everything in their path. Abrahana also talked of Vikings and the warrior Thor. She told us tales of the times her mother and father would visit Norrköping between the two great wars, before travelling on to see friends who worked at the textile mills there. She would pull a face at the mention of pickled herring. We pulled our faces at dried fish with butter and laughed when she confessed to spending a full day running back and forth from the bathroom after eating too much rhubarb pudding.

Sometimes, when Rachel and I were poorly, jealousy would pull us apart—she was always given soup, while I got a dose of syrup of figs. 'If your bowels are open, everything else is okay' Mum would say.

Abrahana would sometimes start speaking in her Swedish tongue, then apologise and begin again in English, laughing at her own stories and memories. Sharing all her tales made her yearn to be back in her homeland. Rachel and I made the promise we would visit her mother's magical city of Stockholm, where we would walk ankle-deep in smiles, dance around poles, singing songs and drinking schnapps, while the children ate so much strawberry cake they could hardly move.

It was one of those days when the rain never stopped. Rachel and I shared an easy chair in the front room, opposite Dad, while she helped me read an Eagle comic. It was a rare day for Mum and Abrahana, who could spend all their time in the kitchen talking, while Dad only left the living room for anything really important, so he could keep an eye on us and how close we were getting.

I never understood why Rachel and her mum kept vanishing. I needed to know what the secret was, and why it was sometimes a full year before we saw each other again.

Rachel and I walked up Blackburn Road and escaped into Astley Bridge Park. It was where we felt most relaxed and could be our true selves. Sitting on the grass near the rose beds behind the bowling shed, we shared our innermost secrets. She would cry at the thought of leaving England, because her mum often talked about returning to Holland, and going to a place where she had no friends, no family. There was no one left. The war had seen to that. After swapping our troubles we were ready again for the real world. We walked across the park to the swings, and I showed off on the monkey bars as she leaned against the park railings, watching life go by.

Henry

Kitty's Diary

He keeps going down to the park to see if Rachel is about.

Within days, she was gone again. I asked where they were. Again, nothing. Just the usual shrug of shoulders. Without Rachel, I decided I needed a pet. Something easy to look after. Dad came home with a tortoise. I called him Henry. He just seemed to look like a 'Henry'. Dad helped make a box, which we filled with straw, for him to play and sleep in. Mum placed some water and food in separate saucers. I overheard Dad say, "Stanley had one for a couple of years," before he started crying. I asked Mum who was Stanley, and why Dad was crying.

"He's not feeling well," she said, before suggesting Dad

go into the kitchen. Without a word he walked away holding his oily handkerchief up to his face. Mum quickly changed the subject, "Henry is a lovely name. Now, you look after him!" I promised I would.

Henry and I became the very best of friends. We played together, and sometimes I would lie down and let him slowly creep over my chest. I often asked Mum about getting a playmate for Henry, but it was always, "Let's see how this works out".

When winter came, Mum reminded me about tortoises needing to hibernate. "He needs to be somewhere nice and warm," she said. I looked all around the house for a box but couldn't find anything suitable. I didn't want him to freeze to death. That would have been so bad for both of us, but *especially* for Henry.

Before going to school, I kissed Henry and placed him in the side oven of our huge, cast-iron range, leaving the oven door ajar. The fire had died out the night before. I was so pleased with myself for thinking of the oven and how lovely and warm it would be for Henry.

It had been a great day: no crying, no bullying, and the teachers had seemed pleased with me. I ran home to see how Henry was getting on with his hibernation. I knew he was going to be so pleased to see me and I would hug and kiss him while I lay on the floor, letting him crawl over me. But, as soon as I saw the oven door closed, I knew there was something wrong. I pulled it open and my arms began to flail. I headbutted the range and ran, screaming, into the back yard, pulled down Mum's washing line, jumped on all the clean clothes and kicked them around the back yard. I found Henry lying on the outside toilet floor after my meltdown was finally over, having forgotten I'd brought him out of the house and into the cool air in the hopes he would suddenly come back to life. On my forehead was a lump the size of an egg.

Even now, all these years later, I still think about how Henry must have suffered, being cooked alive like that. I cried all night that night. Mum came in and rubbed my back for a few minutes, hugged me and wiped my tears, while Dad went for a wet towel for my head.

It was about a week later that I walked in from school to find a birdcage on the kitchen table with a canary inside, bouncing from side to side. Dad spent all evening teaching me how to look after 'George', and we filled his little feeding tubs with Twill bird food. There was something magical about George. Every time I felt like I was going into meltdown, Dad would ask me about George—if he was okay and whether I had bathed him. Dad would have his face up against the cage, whistling to George, and, like magic, he always responded. I would have my face on the opposite side, with Dad encouraging me to try whistling, too. George never responded to me, though. Even so, I kept on trying.

The Secret Room

It was one of the few Saturdays Dad was home. Mum was upstairs, doing all her cleaning stuff, when he asked me to follow him into the best of all the mystery rooms that had always been strictly out of bounds. He lifted out the big bunch of keys from that deep pocket of his, and stressed it was 'our secret'.

"Call it a 'boy thing'," he said, tapping me on the shoulder. Inside the room was a pale red three-piece suite. The walls were white. A shade that looked like a space helmet held a bright lightbulb from the ceiling. On the mantelpiece was a snow shaker, covered in dust, beside a black and white photograph of a boy in long pants, an Alsatian dog beside him. I asked who it was, but there was no answer. More secrets. I moved forward, where my breath misted the front room window.

"See the women walking past," Dad said. "They're all going to the pub. It's a place of evil. Alcohol takes over our entire being and makes you do all the wrong things. Be careful. Alcohol is wrong. It makes you do things you don't want to do."

He sparked up a Woodbine as three Teddy Girls in really tight jeans under bright blue drape jackets and black suede shoes walked past. He stressed how alcohol could trap innocent boys like me. After our chat, Dad let me trampoline from one chair to the other, across the shark-infested waters. I was trying to jump high enough to touch the space helmet hanging from the ceiling, when Mum opened the door. "What have you been telling him?"

He was about to light up again but changed his mind, saying, "I went to court for him," before shouting, "He has to know!"

"Jesus, Mary, and Joseph!" Mum screamed. "What have I brought him into?"

They hurried out into the other room, Mum screaming at Dad, as I carried on trampolining.

Kitty's Diary
Letter
Dear June,

Do you ever see my mother? I wish I were back home—you and me underneath the windmill. Thomas is so strange.

Peter loves him.

9

TEMPERANCE

Dad and I left 339 Blackburn Road just after six that night, bellies full of black pudding and fried eggs. His teeth were in and he wore a clean shirt and tie, his best trilby, and a long navy blue overcoat. He said something about a meeting. It was a ten-minute walk to a red brick building opposite the Iron Church, then through a set of cast-iron railings, and into a room of men with bowler hats and caps—all shapes and sizes, but all black. Around the room, there were colourful banners, taller than our front room. There were large medals: not war medals, but other formal ones. There were introductions, followed by lots of talking and shouting, and songs about the evils of drink.

Dad would be taking me out more and more. Mum was okay with me and Dad becoming closer. At least she knew he wouldn't be taking me into a pub, as other dads would when allowed; not only that, but he also didn't mind me carrying my ball everywhere we went.

Two days later, we caught the Dunscar bus up to the Unknown Soldier cenotaph. I thought all those names etched into the statue were of people laid buried beneath the grass. Dad stepped onto the verge. This was the second time I saw him cry. "They were all pals," he said, holding his black trilby to his chest and muttering about a trench and something or other about gas.

"Whose trench?" I asked. But he kept silent.

Later, we bussed back down to Uncle Harry's. I followed Dad into his brother's bedroom where a near-white skin was covering a skeleton. Mouth wide open, sucking in the ceiling. Dad hurried me back into the front room, where I played with a cannon made from First World War shells that fired matchsticks. There was a strange, dark stink which somehow made me think of the dead cats and dogs I'd seen at the coal furnaces. There was a loud silence about the place, with just a few soft words seeping through. A roaring fire and the cannon kept me company for a while, until I ventured into the bedroom to see the man whose cheeks had disappeared into his mouth, which was wide open and making a strange rasping sound. Dad held his hand. "Harry, it's Tommy." There was a slight flutter of the eyes. "This is Peter," he told him, as Harry returned a forced smile. Maybe it was my imagination, but when Dad said it was me, the eyes seemed to flicker in my direction.

On our way home, Dad shared good times of him with his brother. The months prior to the First World War. About the time they saw the 'monster' who lived at the end of their street—a man who had regularly beaten his wife and kids senseless. The wife had been too afraid to say anything. She didn't think anything would have been done even if she had reported him. Dad said it was Harry's idea to put a piece of dog shit on a drawing pin and stick it onto the thumb latch of the back gate that only the 'monster' used. "We waited on the street corner with a clear view of him. We had to grip our sides to stop ourselves laughing when we saw him prick his thumb on the latch and then shove it straight in his mouth." Dad gave a little shrug of the shoulders. There was a short silence before he added that everyone in the street, even the local copper, had known who razored the monster's face that night as he wobbled home from 'The Duck and Partridge'. He took those scars to the trenches, never to return. Only his mother mourned him. The secret about the razor was kept. Another short silence before Dad laughed a strange laugh, then cried.

On our way home after visiting his dying brother, Dad talked about Eddie Hopkinson. About his transfer from Oldham Athletic to Bolton in 1952, and him being the smallest goalkeeper ever for Bolton and England. It was the best moment ever when he said, "You'll make a great goalkeeper, but, first, you and your ball have to really get to know each other." We had just passed the Iron Church when he took the ball out of my hands and ran halfway down Chalfont Street, turned, and kicked my ball so that it skimmed right over the cobblestones. I bent down for it when he shouted, "No! Hopkinson always gets down on one leg to control the ball; stops the others trying to kick the ball out of your hands. Lots of young goalies make that mistake."

I threw the ball back to him. He trapped it, took control, then somehow reversed it back onto his black boots and kept it up three times before letting it drop to the floor. He side-footed it back to me. "You caught the ball in your hands," he said. "Control it with your chest; get your whole body behind it." I was going to throw it back to him when he put his trilby back over his white hair and said, "You need to keep practising the basics."

He was so good at it, like he'd been doing those moves all his life. His answer when I asked about it was, "It was a long time ago." More secrets. I wasn't understanding why he didn't want to tell me about his footballing past, which there must have been. It was so easy to see, the way he flipped the ball up and twirled it around. I couldn't imagine any other sixty-year-old having those skills unless they'd played to a certain level. Despite the secrets, those few minutes were the best we'd ever spent together. A new father I never knew existed. We practised a single position twenty to thirty times.

Once home, me and ball were soon out the back practising the move Dad had shown us. Hoping that, somehow, once it became second nature, he would come out and show us more. Something strange was happening. I was making me a better me, a more confident me. Somehow, suddenly, I knew where my life was headed. My dream of being a goalkeeper was becoming reality, and Dad was with me all the way.

Saturday 1st March 1958

Bolton v Wolves

My first ever footy match: Quarter-Finals of the F.A. Cup—Bolton v Wolves.

I was still mourning my all-time hero, Duncan Edwards, who had been one of the Busby Babes killed in the Munich air crash on that dreadful February 6th. Dad had found me crying about the crash and, to help take my mind off it, took me to my first ever footy match at Burnden Park.

The queue into Bolton Wanderers v. Wolves was about a half-hour wait. Dad and I stood behind men in dark coats and trilby hats, and other boys my age—clones of their fathers and grandfathers. I couldn't see anyone else dressed like me—in a camel-coloured duffle coat and the multi-

BOLTON WANDERERS
FOOTBALL CLUB

BURNDEN PARK · · · BOLTON

OFFICIAL PROGRAMME 3ᴰ

SEASON 1957-58

F.A. CUP COMPETITION.   SIXTH ROUND
SATURDAY, MARCH 1st

WOLVERHAMPTON W.

Football at Burnden Park next week :
Monday—BURY RES. (7 p.m.) Saturday—BIRMINGHAM C.

coloured balaclava Mum knitted from bits of leftover wools. Some wore leather flying helmets or plain, dark-coloured balaclavas, standing beside their dads who would let them take a sip of their pint of beer. I looked up at Dad shaking his head and tutting as he put his arm around me. He nipped out of the queue to buy me a threepence programme. I'd never had a football programme before.

"Shilling and sixpence for under fourteens." Dad gave me the cash to pay the ticket- when a hand jerked out from behind the glass screen and clawed away my money.

We squeezed and pushed through a blue iron turnstile. It clattered us round into the grounds of Burnden Park where there were more men in long overcoats. Some of them eating hot pies or queuing for beer—shilling and threepence per pint. Some doing both. We made our way to the top stands on the railway end, and stood, watching all the bodies fill up the stadium around us. Dad suggested I go to the toilet before our area was full altogether. I thought I was all right until he added, "If you need to pee, you'll have to hold it, or pee into the person in front's pocket!"

I chose the toilets with yellow-brown walls holding up fifty or more years of urine and covered in rude symbols and drawings of women with their skirts up. A stench of sour pee.

Feeling unsafe and wanting Dad, who was almost invisible in the crowd, I tried to squeeze out through the wall of men.

Thousands of swaying trilbys and bald heads between clouds of cigarette smoke. There were huge chants with black and white scarves waving and rattles rattling along to '*Come on you Bolton*', while the yellow and blacks were trying to drown with '*Wolverhampton, Wolverhampton, we are the champions*'. Arms suddenly punched up through the hubbub, aimed at a man in white jacket carrying a tray with a large sign on the front: **Treacle Toffee 2d a Bag**. He walked round the outside of the pitch, suddenly stopping whenever he saw arms go up, and passed or threw up the bags of toffee into the crowd.

Dad waved his trilby, and a bag was passed to me as he passed 2d down to the man who waved his thanks before moving onto the next arm sticking up among the mass of people. I was squashed up against the man in front when I got lifted up and passed over the tops of hundreds of trilbys, down to the front row, where I waited my turn to be lifted over the barrier with the other kids. We were all safe there, behind the nets, watching the game and stuffing our faces with treacle toffee.

Final score—**Bolton: 2** (Stevens and Parry), **Wolves:1** (Mason).

Once home, my legs ran me faster than fast around the house, stopping just long enough to close all the curtains. Downstairs, the table was sharing steak, chips and peas with us when the excitement took control of me and I started banging out every inch of the game until my brain ran out of words.

Kitty's Diary

Three huge sirloin steaks. 'Treat,' he said, but where from—
how could we ever afford it?

10

DENNIS

June 1958

Not Being Me

Early Sunday morning, Dad was called to the mill on another emergency in the engine room. As always, it was broken ropes halting the machinery for the whole cotton mill and Dad was the only one who could splice all the ropes together. Knowing it was an all-day job, my best clothes got me ready for a day out with Mum to Doncaster to visit a Tomas Feighery. She didn't tell me who he was. We made it up there and back in time for Dad's tea: his favourite Finney haddock. Mum cried nearly all the way home, something that stranger Tomas had said about her 'making her bed'.

I wanted to know *what* bed, and why the man had started crying when he saw me. I never found out.

A perfect day, walking round and round the school playground on my own, every so often standing to look through the cast iron railings into Astley Bridge Park. Easy. For a reason I've never been able to explain—perhaps a moment of madness—I asked Tony Banks, Michael Gordon, Freddy Ambit, and Dennis Hughes if they wanted to meet my new puppy dog, who I had called Vick after my Dad's big Alsatian who had died a few years before.

Vick freaked all over them, even managing to lick Tony Bank's face. Tony was taller than Dad. I was trying too hard to be one of them. I'd been having a difficult day when I wanted to be like them, be in their gang. I was showing off in the middle of a wrestling match with Vick when his back legs separated directly over my face. I went to lift him off but then he peed all over me. They laughed. They laughed all the way out of my house. They carried that tale and laughter back into school, infecting the other kids and even the teachers. Only Dennis hadn't laughed. Maybe because I never laughed at him when the teacher pointed him out for wearing only a vest in school and had made him put on his jacket. He had tried to tell her there were no shirts at home, but she dismissed it as some excuse: 'Everyone has more than one shirt'. Dennis was made to stay in the classroom and I had sneaked back in to keep him company and console his embarrassment.

***

Dennis and his dad were standing next to each other on Mum's freshly-scrubbed, donkey-stoned shiny doorstep and all pumped, ready to invite me on a picnic in Barrow Bridge.

Five miles later, Barrow Bridge Lane parted enough for us to see another world where wooden bridges were walking young and old over a stream towards stone cottages selling ice cream. Behind us, dozens of families with kids, all smaller clones of their parents, in colourless clothes; men and boys with Brylcreemed hair and axed partings; women with rouged cheeks and hair set with clips, in below-knee skirts or dresses. On the football pitch-sized boating lake there were families in various creaky, wooden boats rowing and paddling around the big yellow jumper man. In a kind of order, they edged towards the side of the lake without protest and soon were out, making way for the next set of punters' threepence ten-minute rides. There was cheering and nervous laughter when they were finally on the water, the excitement of rowing on that lake for ten minutes to wherever the boats wanted to take them. A sense of freedom being in the countryside and clean air. None of that sickly smell of the cotton mill. Everyone in dreamland until the megaphone blasted, "Number twenty-five, your time is up!"

There was another surge forward when the yellow jumper went to collect the money. He repeated this over and over, giving all the families a chance.

Once back on dry land, we walked past the last stone houses of Barrow Bridge and up the lane towards Scout Road. We stopped a few seconds for a spitting competition into a lazy stream, which I won; but Dennis, not happy at being beaten, won our peeing competition. The side lane walked us up through overhanging branches, the stream on our far right, and we carried on into the woods. Mr. Heaton, Dennis' dad, found a patch of grass round about the size of half a penalty area, and waved us away while he rested with his book. We pushed our way through the bracken and hanging branches, scrambling over huge boulders where we played war games. Dennis, a Commando, searching for me, a Foreign Agent. I became invisible behind a thick tree as he loaded his machine gun, and I jumped out to kill him with my rubber dagger. After, it was my turn to be Commando, and my turn to be killed with that same dagger.

Once our excitement wore off, we both collapsed, laying still for a while until we saw a Messerschmitt flying overhead and blasted it with our machine guns. We imagined the German pilot parachute down and run through the dark woods. Dennis suggested playing hide and seek. I closed my eyes and counted to twenty. "Coming, ready or not!" I was suddenly lost in the middle of everywhere. Panic was setting in as I stumbled around searching for myself. I needed to know where I was and why everything looked so different. I was in some other land, far from where I had just been with Dennis.

"I'm over here," he shouted. I didn't know where 'over here' *was*. I didn't know where *anything* or *anywhere* was. I was lost inside my own head. I fell to the ground screaming and crying with anger. I wanted to kill everything. Dennis came over and knelt beside me. He didn't shout. He didn't ask me how I was. Instead, he just waited until my meltdown eased away. Minutes later, after the explosion in my head had gone, I was ready to be me again. With our war games over, we kicked clumps of mushrooms and toadstools to death, then scrambled over boulders carried downstream from ancient quarries. We came to the top of Barrow Bridge, almost level with the famous '63 Steps', and looked down on Bolton and the dozens of factory chimneys.

Almost back to base camp, we took off our socks and shoes and walked downstream. Our toes bumped apart standing over the pebbles as smoke from our dinner, seeping through the woods like a search party, caught our nostrils. We could hear the bacon and eggs applauding in the frying pan.

We enjoyed our meal, resting against a fallen tree trunk. We talked parents, school, football, and camping, and how much we had loved those few hours away from the boring everyday.

Strange; after that, Dennis never came back to school. There was no answer when I knocked on their front or back door. The once-white curtains which had seen better days were closed. I never saw him again. Even our teachers didn't know where Dennis had gone to. Every time I asked, it was the shrug of the shoulders.

11

SECRETS AND MONSTERS

339 Blackburn Road, Bolton, was full of secrets. Every room in the house seemed to hold one. There were secrets on the shelf above the kitchen door, and I found more in the form of big leather-toed football boots covered in dust, but too small for my size six feet. I really liked the pen knife with its ivory cover, and a tiepin in the shape of an Alsatian dog. Again, there were no answers to my many questions, made even worse with Mum saying I had to forget about them. I wouldn't want to be anywhere near them again because of the cold breathing coming from something alive down there in the dark cellar. The cold breathing which always hit my bare legs whenever I stepped out of the kitchen and hurried past the cellar door opposite. A warning? What else? Whatever *was* down there, only Dad could control it. I was

still in two minds when he said I could stay at the top of the steps while he went down to whatever it was. He took the bunch of keys that he kept in those deep pockets of his, chose the small one and whistled the dust off it. There was creaking from the doorframe trying to hold the door back, until Dad pulled it open. Before my eyes could focus, he closed the door behind him, slotting a heavy bar across the door to prevent me from opening it and trying to go down into the cold breath of something I definitely didn't want to see or meet. Just a split-second peep convinced me I saw the shape of a human being. That night, my imagination carried it around into something so frightening I woke up crying. I clutched my new rosary, proving once again I was a true Catholic, as I believed it would protect me from monsters, tuberculosis, or anything else the world might throw at me. Suddenly the bulge of four overcoats hanging on the back of my door for dear life, from my bed, looked like a hunchback was hanging on it.

Kitty's Diary

August 1958

Those same men who brought the nearly new gas cooker and biggest oven I have ever seen brought us a set of almost new pans.

After making breakfast, ball and I bounced our way up Blackburn Road towards Astley Bridge Park where the grassed acre was readying itself for the big trample of a hundred kids or so. We were lying down, just yards from the drinking fountain, wondering about nothing in particular, when a plane thousands of feet above us was passed from one cloud to the other. I wondered where in America my auntie Annie lived, and I so wished I was on that plane, so I could thank her for the gift of cowboy boots and shirt she had sent over.

There was something really nice about me and ball just lying there in silence, except for the imagined roar of the plane and the white clouds of vapour trailing it. Where did all that white stuff come from?

Maybe it was the sense of freedom that made me feel dozy—I don't think I fell asleep, otherwise I wouldn't have seen Mike Warren, in his Man United top, walk up and stand over me to ask for a kickabout. First it was a warm-up with the ball. Then others turned up, as though they'd been hidden behind the rows of rhododendrons all along. Shirts for goal posts. "Street's in goal," Curtis called out. Ball was zooming in from every direction; I was diving everywhere, tipping it over the top of an imagined crossbar or fingertipping the shots around the side post. Watching them dribble the ball and all come together, as though it were some strange dance, confirmed the lonely place for me in goal, standing there alongside my Eddie.

Half-time was spent gulping a threepence bottle of Tizer's Dandelion and Burdock. And when all the legs were aimed for home and food, I lay down near the water fountain, hoping the aeroplane I saw earlier might be on its way back.

***

I left ball sunbathing in the corner of our back yard in those last days of that 1958 hot summer school holiday, because Mum wanted us to spend more time 'out and about'. That usually meant catching the number 55 up into Belmont. We would stand and marvel at the Belmont Yachting Club as the highly-coloured sails puffed and billowed, their tall poles puncturing the blue sky. From her leather bag, she would take out a tea towel bulging with spam sandwiches, and we would rest there on the side of the road; just me and Mum, not another soul nearby. I would stroke her red hair as she held me. Sometimes I was so happy, I would cry. Whatever happened, our picnics always ended with Lucozade.

Half an hour walked us over to the Black Dog pub where beer sniffed my nose. Then it was a visit to the Blue Lagoon reservoir, where Mum let me take off my shoes and socks, carefully gripping the back of my jumper as she pointed left to a black jetty stretching out over the water. It had a bad reputation for taking young boys not much older than me. Boys, boasting to their girlfriends, had run and jumped off into the freezing water, which was always happy to be relieved of its boredom. Waves ready to catch the unsuspecting boys, gripping tight their struggles, while the freeze, in partnership with the water, would reach up from the depths and pull them miles down, shackling them to the bottom, never to be seen again.

I was only ankle-deep when she pulled me back. "That's as far as you go!" I had never known *anything* so cold. Like putting my feet into a bucket of ice. "It's very dangerous!"

"But *they're* swimming and jumping in!"

"*They'll* regret it, or their *parents* will for letting them in there on their own!"

I had never seen her looking so frightened. Mum took out a little bottle of water splashed some onto her fingers and then crossed my forehead, saying out loud, "In the name of the Father, the Son, and the Holy Ghost. Amen." We said our prayers and then she announced that she should like it if I became a parish priest, but that, first, I really needed to learn how to look after myself. "No old crow will be looking after you." After drying our feet, we went off to have our butties.

"We'll start with sewing," she said. "You must always have a button box." I knew *all* about Mum's button box from the time my button came off my trousers and she had shown me how to find the 'right' button and sew it back on. Everything was with priesthood in mind. I had to learn the 'little jobs', as she called it. Mum had put her hand in the tin box and brought out the first button she touched. Whatever size or colour it was, that was the button she would use, regardless. Yes, the other kids made fun of my yellow button, just as they had with the zip-up winter bootees. At least she didn't force me to wear anything that was mocked. I think school became a kind of testing ground for all of Mum's fashion ideas. I often thought she was a frustrated designer. Especially after the six-foot, double-layered red, black and yellow scarf she knitted from old jumpers found at rummage sales. She even upcycled them into socks and gloves. The crème de la crème was a scarf that I could push up inside itself and turn into a bob hat and scarf. Okay, it never really left our house. It looked so modern, so futuristic, that I was too frightened to wear it.

Kitty's Diary
October 1958

Peter cleaned up his dad's dysentery. Bloody diarrhoea in the potty. Emptied it out the back toilet.
He shouldn't be doing it, but I have to work. Six weeks, school not asked after him.

Those few dysentery weeks, my job was to give Dad the doctor's medicine, plus a boiled egg, with its shell, crushed, in a cup with butter, salt, and pepper—which Uncle David promised would put a lining on Dad's stomach. Between giving his medicine, I would go outside where me, ball, and the wall would get it together. In those few weeks, he still went on about temperance, with warnings about alcohol turning people into monsters.

Kitty's Diary

More strange men visiting to see how he is, and presents for Peter.

A few mornings later, Dad, in his chair, gripping a pint of tea in his left hand while a Woodbine cigarette banged his lungs, gave me money for Moss Street Baths.

I jumped in with flippers and a mask and swam underwater while pretending I was Lloyd Bridges in 'Sea Hunt'. Taking my best deep breaths, I would swim down into my own world where I saw boats sinking and people holding out their hands to be rescued. I would bob up for an extra-deep breath, then dive back down nine feet to touch the bottom, before shooting back up for another breath.

Ghost

Warily walking through our open front door, I called, "Hello?" The house seemed more still and silent than ever before. "Hello? Mum, Dad? Anyone home?"

I wanted to leave, but couldn't. The stairs were silent of creaks. So, too, was the landing walking me into my bedroom.

My house was dying.

I went downstairs looking for Vick, who was usually all over me after being away most of the day, when suddenly, making me jump, "You're late," said Mum from behind the kitchen door. She beckoned me into the best room, where she lifted a white dust-sheet that had the shape of a ghost lying on the carpet, right there at my feet. Gone, were the rusty innards from an old two-wheeler bike, now feeling sorry for themselves. Standing proud were handlebars, holding out for a pair of hands, and a freshly-oiled chain. Close by, brake blocks, begging for some action. So, too, were the reflectors, seat, dynamo, and even new pedals. Dad laid out various sized spanners and screwdrivers. He sat me down and I watched as he put it all together. He didn't say a word. Then he just lit up a Woodbine and that was that. I was crying with joy and excitement as Dad threw all the old bits into the middle of the ghost sheet, tied up the four corners, carried the lot out over his shoulder, and let it crash down by the dustbin.

Kitty's Diary

Strangers asking about Peter. Why? He's not done anything wrong.

Dad stood outside for a few minutes before walking over to the back gate. He did nothing but stand there, looking left and right. I don't know what, or who, he was looking for, but he killed two Woodbines while he was at it. I watched him spark up another, and, like Bogart, he let it dangle from the side of his mouth while blowing out smoke from between his tight, thin lips. It looked as though he was going to say something. But he didn't.

I asked him where the bike had come from.

Silence.

I never found out.

It was the best bike in our neighbourhood.

Kitty's Diary

November 1958

He's bought me a new watch after fixing Mr. Cohen's drains.

12

HOLLYWOOD

The four of us—Mum, Dad, me, and my bike—made our way down to Tippings Brew. The bike was holding Mum's hand when Dad, for whatever reason, started talking about old Hollywood film stars. He spoke of Tom Mix, Fatty Arbuckle, Charlie Chaplin, and James Cagney as though he knew them all personally. He told me about how Tom Mix was a really good friend of the real Wyatt Earp, and how Mix had cried when Earp's cortège was going through the town. He even told me how Fatty Arbuckle had gotten into trouble with some woman. Whatever it was, Arbuckle had managed to get away with it, but was never seen in films again. Dad was in the middle of telling me something about James Cagney when he held on tight to the seat of my bike and told me to climb on.

Kitty's Diary

Saturday mornings they sit and watch 'The Ring'. Boxing's no good for him.

I tried and tried to ride it, but I just kept falling off. I wasn't the only one who wanted to go home: my bike was just stretched out on the floor; not even an inch of wheel was moving. Dad picked it up, wiped off the dirt and polished the seat with a duster from his pocket. The bike walked him back over to me. It was the way both of them stood next to each other waiting for me to do whatever; it was the way he held the seat. It sounds crazy, but somehow, it was like they knew each other. Dad retold the James Cagney story about how he had ducked real live bullets in the film *Angels with Dirty Faces*. I didn't understand why he was telling me the same thing over and over again. He had never done this before. In fact, he had never really talked about Cagney before, except to say that he was a fabulous dancer who'd had a very poor upbringing. Dad pointed over at Mum, saying, "Cagney's mum was Irish too." I never found out how he knew all that stuff about celebrities and movie stars.

Kitty's Diary

Peter's upset because his teacher made Michael Warren stay in the classroom, and some other kid was given Michael's position on the pitch.

I wasn't sure what Dad meant by it. Again and again, he kept telling me the Cagney story. He also told me that before special effects, the filmmakers used army or police snipers to fire at the upstairs windows in the film, and how one live bullet had just grazed Cagney.

While my mind was on that Cagney story, Dad let go of my seat and my bike took charge, peddling my legs round and round, whizzing me down the road where Mum was screaming, "Slow down!" Suddenly, I found my bike and I had become the best of friends, both of us enjoying the thrill of it all. Together. As one. Not only that, but the pedals seemed even more excited than I was, whizzing round like they did, but tiring my legs. Regardless, all my fear had been pedalled away. I could see a Woodbine banging Dad's lungs as he tipped his hat back like Bogart and waited for us to slow up.

When my bike and I had had enough, we stopped, and I ran over to Dad and jumped into his arms. Then, for some reason, he started to cry. Mum said he had a bad cold, but I knew it was more than that. I could see the bike was just as tired as me, lying down the way it did.

Kitty's Diary
On his own, all that way up to Moss Bank Park.

The bike went home with Mum while Dad took me to

celebrate in Jack Sheff's Temperance Bar, Waterloo Street, close to Empire Cinema where we had watched Charlie Chaplin in 'Gold Rush'. Chaplin had eaten his own black boots, but Dad later explained that the boot was made of liquorice.

It was nettle beer at Jack Sheff's. Dad slotted money into the jukebox: Tommy Steel's 'Singing the Blues', Jerry Lee Lewis' 'Great Balls of Fire', and Johnny Ray's 'Just Walking in the Rain'. They talked cricket, about the England squad with Captain Peter May, and it being the best England team to face The Old Enemy in Australia. "The Ashes are ours!" exclaimed Jack Sheff.

Kitty's Diary

...And who is that Jack Johnson he always talks about?

They were all talking and laughing when Dad suddenly said, "You know they tried shooting Jack Johnson after he won the world championship title". The two stopped talking and listened as Dad spoke of Jack Johnson, the first black world champion boxer, and how people had tried to assassinate him because of his colour. Then, without warning, he jumped up and started shadow-boxing. I'd never seen a black man before. Other people in the bar came and listened to him talk about this first black boxer, and then about the Olympic champion Jesse Owens, at the Hitler Games.

On the way home, people were waving and calling to Dad from across the road. He called and waved back. We went into one of the pawn shops where he shook hands with a tall man wearing a big, gold pocket watch dangling over his belly. I recalled the time Mum and I had carried a bucket of coal on the bus to this strange man who went by the name Maxi.

They were both looking into one of the many glass cases when Dad said, "That one," pointing to a Hopalong Cassidy wristwatch. Maxi lifted the lid and gave it to me. No money was handed over. Dad never paid out money to anyone, especially not the pawnshops. That was the day when Maxi handed Dad a large leather bag and I watched, open-mouthed, as the bag was filled with watches, both pocket and wristwatches, a few gold, but mostly silver. Some dirty coins and medals, too, which had been polished to make them look more valuable than they actually were. I followed Dad and Maxi into the back room—an Aladdin's cave of every household good you might need. Dad reminded Maxi it was getting time to check his drains if he wanted to prevent another blockage stink like the one that happened last time.

Kitty's Diary
Peter spending most of his time at the pictures. It's not good for a boy—he should be out with the others.

I always found it strange when I heard other kids or their grown-ups saying, 'this cost *this* much' or 'that cost *so* much'. I could never remember Mum or Dad saying anything like that. Mum was always taking me down to the shops in Bolton to get new clothes. I had clothes galore. If I needed new football boots, I was walked to the sports shop down Blackburn Road. As soon as we entered the shop, the owner would ask, 'How's Tommy?' Then on our way out he would always say, 'Give him my regards'.

It was strange how everyone seemed to know him and absolutely never was a bad word said against him.

I was safe.

13

CHRISTMAS

Coupons

It was always beginning of December when we would start counting and preparing coupons in exchange for goods.

Mum, Rachel and I were cross-legged on the carpet cutting out the Black and Greens family tea tokens, Mum driving us potty, singing the Black and Greens tea advert:

> *Have you ever stopped to think*
> *How many cups of tea you drink,*
> *How many cups of tea a day,*
> *How many packets thrown away?*
> *Think of all the gifts this means*
> *If you were drinking Black & Greens!*

I tried using scissors to cut around the labels and in a straight line, the way Rachel and Mum were doing it.

They made it look so easy. I found it difficult to even follow the dotted line. I didn't understand why it was all so difficult for me, but so easy for them. We had laid out newspapers to stop the tea from covering the carpet, and, when we were done, we threw the pile of leaves into the coal fire.

Whoooosh.

"You'll know it if you set the chimney on fire because the fire brigade will soon come and sort it," shouted Mum. "Now, stack the tokens into lines of ten."

I found it difficult to place them in the order Mum wanted. I tried and tried. Rachel showed me how, but I just couldn't get it right. After the first two or three stacks, it all started to go wrong again. My head seemed to be changing. My head felt heavy and my thinking went off somewhere. I wanted to say something but my brain had vanished. I couldn't. So I stacked the tokens by feel and look. The stacks looked fine to me, until Rachel started rearranging them in nice, neat lines, all boasting ten tokens high. There were enough tokens for Mum's kitchen clock. She congratulated us and Rachel leaned over and kissed me.

I was smiling a perfect smile when Dad asked, "Is that your mum shouting for you?"

I couldn't hear anything, but Rachel's coat was already on and she was out the door, headed for the top of Raby Street to meet her mum.

There was an angry silence before Mum shouted, "There's

nothing wrong with the girl."

Then, as usual, Dad responded with, "I went to court for him!"

It was two days before there was a civil tongue between them and the house was at ease again.

Washing Up

Saturday's kitchen was like a Turkish bath, with steam rising out of a dolly-tub and Mum bent over it, using the block of Fairy soap to scrub Dad's blue overalls. They were too big for the washing machine. She'd grab hold of Dad's navy blue work shirts, lift them out and punch the hell out of all the bubbles, then hold them under the water until all sign of air was gone. She would wring them and slip them into the corner where I would wind them through the 'squeezers'.

There were more gadgets for her kitchen when Dad heard or saw of anything which could make housework life easier. Every time she would ask where or how he had come about them, but there was never any real answer.

Secrets.

His wage was about ten pounds per week. So, how? Even with overtime, he wouldn't have been able to afford it. I didn't understand why so many men, complete strangers, would come to our house and leave whatever they were carrying on the table or sideboard. Sometimes, they would disappear down into the cellar and stay for hours; sometimes, they were there nearly all weekend. Some who came wore tweeds and drove posh cars. There were others who, like Uncle David, would bring strange things, like buckets with holes in the bottom. The strangest by far was a real live monkey which I wasn't allowed anywhere near. The monkey in the cage only stayed for a couple of hours before it was gone. There never seemed to be any money handed over. Yet Dad always had enough money to last us. I cannot remember any one time when Dad or Mum ever mentioned being short of it.

One Saturday—Dad in his comfy chair watching the week's boxing match and flicking cigarette ash onto the carpet (even though an ashtray was in reach); Mum getting the dolly tub out; and me playing out back—two strangers walked up. A man with jet black hair, like mine, and a blonde woman. They stopped and watched me for a second, before the man kicked the bottom of the gate that Dad had been meaning to mend and went into the house. There were shouts, screams, and swearing, banging my ears.

Out came the woman, drenched from head to foot, and Mum behind her, carrying the empty washing-up bowl. Water everywhere. Screams everywhere.

Kitty's Diary
NO ONE calls my Peter a little bastard!

14

SPACEMEN

January 1959

In school, the teachers were telling us we had to sleep with
our arms crossed over our chest to make sure that, if we
died in our sleep, we would go straight to Heaven. I tried
and tried, but I couldn't get to sleep like that. It just kept me
awake thinking: if I wasn't going to Heaven, where *would* I
go? I really tried sleeping as was asked of me. I just couldn't.
I would wake up with my arms at my sides or partly under
my pillow, everywhere except over my chest. When I told
the teacher, she hit me between the eyes with, 'If you don't
go to sleep like that, your wishes of becoming a goalkeeper
won't happen'. I never tried to sleep with my arms across
my chest ever again, because I thought that if Jesus was so

uncaring, then I didn't want to know.

Once home, I didn't play my usual game of footy with the stairs, who stood waiting patiently for it to happen. I was too traumatised by the teacher's comments. When Mum came home unexpectedly, she found me in Dad's chair in floods of tears. Between sobs, I explained what had been said. Within minutes, she had written a letter I was to take, requesting a meeting with the headmaster.

There would never be a response.

Trying to make me feel better, while mopping up the puddle of tears, she promised we would go for our walk over the moors that coming weekend.

***

Saturday afternoon, as promised, was our day out, and after much pestering we made for the Belmont moors, north of Bolton. Those moors walked us through enough wild heathers to fill a football pitch. Suddenly, tall floodlights surrounding us lit up a huge building and some strange, glowing, tall men, each of them with bright heads and bodies coloured in red, blue, yellow, and green hues. They were all leaning against the tall security fence, drinking from tin mugs and sharing fags.

"Hello, Kitty," one of the spacemen shouted from a few yards away. "And how is Thomas Edgar? This will be Peter, then?"

"Stop staring," whispered Mum, turning to me.

They talked about Dad and the mill, and whether he was thinking about retiring. They pushed their faces against the fence; it was the first time I had ever seen spacemen up close. They were looking me in the eye. One of them snarled, making me jump back. Mum laughed.

There was a long silence while everyone just focused on me, when, finally, Mum said goodbye and walked me away.

One of them aimed a weird face at me, his belly bulging through the gaps in the fence, and called, "Tell your Dad the moon men have been asking after him." Fright quickly grabbed and pulled me away from those five aliens.

Once we reached the top of the hill and turned round, we could still see their glowing frames. They looked even bigger than when we had been just inches from them. They seemed to be looking up at us. I was so relieved seeing them still behind the high fence.

It was a long walk home. Mum was still going strong; I was tired, but not tired enough not to ask once more why we couldn't walk along Scout Road, where you could see the army shooting range. It was the only time I heard her shout, "No." I asked again. There came another resounding, "No." And it was the only time she hit me hard enough for the whack to get through my jacket arm. I don't know who was the most shocked, me or Mum!

We headed past Scout Road, and the red flag waving danger, where I would usually pester her to let me see the soldiers practising their shooting skills. She grabbed my pointing hand and, without even looking, led me down the narrow lane toward Barrow Bridge.

Kitty's Diary
Those red flags flapping. All my fault.

Choking back her tears, she kept asking if I was okay. There was a short silence before she said sorry, kissed me, and rubbed away her whack. She ripped some heather and put a piece in my buttonhole and the rest in her bag. She told me it was good luck, for a long life, and then hugged and kissed me again.

It was always there and never let me down. Yes, there were times when I ignored it, and this was one of those days. The toilet understood it would still be there, doing nothing except stand there at the bottom of the yard side, waiting for me and another game of marbles. My toilet friend. My space, my playground, ever since a posh one was fitted upstairs. A space I could share with the old toilet bowl, now retired and doing nothing but sitting there, reading strips of the Bolton Evening News strung to the wooden door. A place where I could practice my marble skills.

A Step Forward

Kitty's Diary

February 1959

He's bought Peter another pair of football boots.
Different from the other ones, more like shoes. Fancy with
red and black stripes either side.

My mind kept going over my first football match, and
goalkeeper Eddie Hopkins, who had become my hero. A *real*
hero. I could see him in the Bolton nets and, if I was lucky
enough, get his autograph when he came out of the grounds
with Freddy Hill and Tommy Banks.

Not My Real Birthday

Strange how Mum and Dad decided Whit Sunday would be
a good day for my birthday. I think Mum planned it that
way because all the Catholic schools would be parading the
streets of Bolton. That morning, still in my pyjamas and
wiping the sleep from my eyes, Dad came over to kiss my
forehead and wish me happy birthday.

Yes, it was good having presents. Yes, it was exciting
having a birthday. Better still was Mum's homemade jam
roly-poly cake with candles spiked out from every angle.

It was something to behold. My real birthday was Christmas Day. I was getting the best of everything. I wanted new football boots most of all; flippers and goggles for Moss Street Baths would have been good; a signed Peter May cricket bat was what I prayed for.

Instead, I was given a brand-spanking-new blue and white school uniform for when I went up to the big school— St. Anne's Secondary Modern, Stitch-Mi-Lane, Harwood. It was two sizes too big, but instead of taking it back for a smaller size, Mum just folded up all the cuffs and hems, saying I would grow into it. When I said everyone in my year would be wearing a brand-new uniform, she laughed. "That's daft of them. Why pay out all that money for a new uniform when they'd never wear it again!"

Kitty's Diary
June 1959

*He's brought oiled bobbins home; we're showing Peter how
to chop and tie them into bundles.
6d a bundle to sell on the street corner.*

Dad had Mum teach me how to bundle up oil-soaked bobbins to sell on the street corner. Then came the big surprise: Dad giving Mum enough money to take us to Blackpool during Wakes Week. He said he was too busy to leave the factory even for that holiday week. Mum had never set foot in a posh hotel, never mind stayed in one. It wasn't one of those very posh ones, where everyone dresses up for meals, but it was still posh. The table was set out, silver service style, and waiters came and asked her if she wanted a glass of wine. She declined. Some of the other parents seemed puzzled at how the table was laid. It was Mum who explained which spoon to use for soup and how to work from the outside in. Even now, all these years later, I still remember the faces around that table with its fancy tablecloth and serviettes.

We spent rainy days in the Tower Ballroom watching circus and dance acts, Reginald Dixon on an organ rising up out of the ground. Then it was Madame Tussauds, where we saw murderer John Haigh, the Acid Bath killer. Mum told me about the serial killer John Christie. I asked why she was crying, and she told me about someone called Derek Bentley who had been wrongfully convicted and executed for the murder of a policeman. Downstairs, in a darker-than-dark room, there were Japanese and British prisoners of war with huge stomachs, forced out, further than a nine-month pregnant woman, with water. Then there was the drip-dripping of water onto the forehead of another prisoner. I was both excited and frightened, and wanted to go around again. "No," Mum said.

Kitty's Diary
July 1959

Even in Blackpool, Peter's pressing those bloody telephone box buttons like his dad to try and get a threepence back.

We shared the beach with deckchairs, balloons, white knotted handkerchiefs, lobster-coloured arms and legs, and goodness knows what else. There were donkeys, kiss-me-quick hats, and hundreds of noses all sniffing out fish and chips. All the other kids were either laughing or crying, pointing at the Punch and Judy show. I didn't understand what was happening.

I was sat on the sand with my ball, resting after a hectic kickabout, when three boys asked if I wanted a game. Mum nodded. I went in goal. The ball came in fast to the left-hand corner, just inside our coats for goalposts. I dived and fingertipped the ball round the other side of the post, just as Eddie would have done. "Save!" shouted one of the boys.

I did three more Eddie saves before Mum said she wanted to move on, but then a man picked up the ball and kicked it for the goal.

Saved!

Annoyed, he handed his can of beer to his mate before slamming in another ball. I leaped to my right and tipped it round the imaginary post. There were more shouts of 'Save!' as he tried six more times and gave up, walking off, booze in hand.

Kitty's Diary

August 1959

Bloody hell. New wallpaper. New carpets. New Hoover.

Back home, the walls had been decorated with flowery wallpaper, and the paintwork sanded down and repainted white. Dad was leaning against the wall, banging a Woodbine and looking ever so pleased with himself. But he couldn't understand why Mum was crying. They were 'happy tears'.

15

BIG SCHOOL

Four glorious weeks, I was in goal on Astley Bridge Park, and it felt so natural. Every time I tried to play out of goal, I often fell over the ball because it wouldn't move for me. It was more like a *cannon*ball than a *foot*ball. Everyone else would be running up and down as the ball enjoyed dancing between their feet, doing more or less everything asked of it. Okay, at times it was stubborn and did its own thing, straying everywhere except where it was asked to go. It was during those few weeks I realised my life was going to be in goal: that was it and life was going to get better and better.

Mum often came searching for me. Three times she turned up at the park; three times I was embarrassed. She freaked at the idea of me not being able to tell her what time I'd be home. I could only say I'd be back when the game was over.

She tried her best in understanding, but she couldn't get over worrying about me. She would come sit beside me on the back step, watching the other kids play in the back street, doing their own thing. I never understood the cause for my shaking body, the tightness in my chest, or my fast breathing. I would end up in the back yard toilet playing marbles.

***

One of those 1959 summer nights walked me and Vick, my black mongrel dog, along a cobbled road from Tippings Brew all the way down to the power station, where a narrow, concrete bridge walked us over the river. We passed through the long grass and tall wildflowers who were nodding a welcome. Well, it was mostly willow herb—that's probably why everyone called them the 'cotton fields', because of all the cotton-looking seeds. Onward we went, past a triangle of clinkers the size of bus shelters that we all thought had fallen from space. It's where Vick and I lay on the grass in the shade of a bunch of small trees, a few yards from those fishing by the four lodges.

In our secret place, where no one could see or hurt us, we watched a gang of Teddy Boys and Girls smoking and hurling stones through the deserted factory windows. I tried clasping Vick's jaws together when he started to bark, but he shook his barks out of my hand and bounced up and down, barking even louder. The gang approached us with studded belts and flick knives, ready for whatever trouble was going to jump out at them. We crawled out from underneath the trees and ran. I was pulling Vick while he tried to turn back and charge at the gang, now running and pelting us with stones. They jeered and cursed as they gained in on us, from maybe fifty yards away, as we crossed the bridge onto Tippings Brew. I couldn't think of what I might say if they caught us, except to swear that I wouldn't speak a word about them or their stones to *anyone*. They finally backed off when a Warburtons bread van sped down the hill toward the bakery depot just in time to rescue us. Breathlessness leaned me against the Hesketh's cotton mill wall as I gathered my thoughts and what-ifs…

Half an hour later, we were safely home, and I was peeling potatoes and cutting perfect-sized chips to partner three sausages and an egg. Then it was an hour sat on the back step, toying with a choice of kickabout with the wall or marbles out in the back toilet. Marbles won.

Bogart

That summer of '59 brought warm mornings after rainy nights, and hot afternoons. I would lie down on the grass of Astley Bridge Park and watch the birds and planes being passed from cloud to cloud. It was on one of those days that I returned home to find two plain clothes detectives, dressed like Bogart, waiting inside to speak to me.

"You've gone white," said the detective with a notepad in one hand and fag in the other.

While he waited for me to answer, a big lump of fright bloated my stomach and a ball of words, "I was in school," stuck in my throat.

From behind the fag in his mouth, he said, "Was it you who climbed through your Mum's window? The shoe marks look about your size."

I shrugged my shoulders. I knew what I wanted to say, but my brain wasn't giving my mouth permission to speak my thoughts. Dad was leaning against the wall while Mum brought in cups of tea on a tray swimming with her tears.

"Where have you been all day while your parents have been out?"

"Eh, just a minute!" Dad said. "That's my son, you don't talk to him like that. It wouldn't have been him who climbed in through the back window and tried to jimmy open the cellar door."

"Now you mention the cellar. What's down there?" asked the man. Mum crashed her eyes into Dad's.

"Nothing, really. Just bits and bats like draining rods, handy things you keep in cellars." Dad took out his keys

133

and whistled away the dust, asking, "Do you need to look?" Mum's face was white.

The fag in the cop's mouth moved to one side letting out, "No, that's all right."

They shrugged their shoulders, looked at each other, banged their eyes into me and then said their goodbyes.

"You and that cellar!" Mum shouted at Dad, before wrapping her arms around me.

"They've caught him in Blackpool," the detective called by to tell them two days later.

***

September 1959

I didn't understand why Mum was teary, but she said something about losing me. That Sunday morning, Mum and I went to Mass and Communion. Other kids from my old school were clocking in, too, for the nine o'clock service. The kids I had shared those first years with were now all getting ready to make the journey together into big school.

I was the only one without a basin haircut, greased with a white parting axed down one side. Yes, I wanted to look like all the other kids, but deep down, I really wanted my hair like Uncle David's. The rough look. I longed to know his secret:

to be able to run my fingers through my hair just like he did, and for my hair to do exactly what it was told; as opposed to just doing its own thing when and however it wanted, like lying flat on my forehead, depressed, pretending to be dead; or up in the air like it had been on speed all night.

Before our big school day, Mum took charge of my hair situation. "A practice run," she called it, sitting me down in the big chair facing the fireplace. She went about fixing it in the same way she did her cakes: whizzing through it and hoping for the best. Somehow, it always worked— well, *nearly* always. Dad and I were always amazed at the incidental way she went about doing everything, as though she had a magic wand under that apron of hers. This is how she went about sorting my hair too. Nothing planned. No discussions. She whizzed here and there with the scissors, while Dad nodded his approval like it was her licence to carry on doing whatever she was doing in her very own way, regardless of the consequences. That Saturday was no exception. After barbering my head, she fingered a lump of Vaseline from its tin, melted it in her palms and rubbed it into my hair, before combing it into an original 'Catherine Street' hairdo that ended up somewhere between a 'Gene Vincent' and a wilder 'Jerry Lee Lewis' after playing 'Great Balls of Fire!'.

I had to sit in the chair until the Vaseline set. For one day, and one day only, my hair did as it was told. Frightened,

I didn't move an inch the whole time. 'Not conforming' is what Mum called it. Dad called it "Being stubborn—an Irish thing!"

"Well, it's better than being English." I thought there was going to be some great fallout. I had never known them shout out that sort of thing before.

I tried complaining about my hair, to calm things down. "You are not *everyone else*. You are Peter Street." There was no answer to that, so Mum won again. Well, I suppose I did, too. Dad didn't mind either way.

Day One at St. Anne's

All the new kids for St. Anne's had to wait down by the side of Manley Terrace, near Astley Bridge Park on Crompton Way, for the school bus.

It was then that fright kicked in.

Mum had arranged with Mrs. Kelly that I would go to the big school that first week with her two sons: David, who was on his last year, and his younger brother, Sean, who was just a couple of weeks younger than me. Sean and I were friends from junior school, but he never got on too well with my wall. He was more into fishing. Vick and I would sometimes meet him while he fished by the four lodges down Tippings Brew. It was there where I first met his brother, David, who had looked at me and said, "I could piss on your friend and drown him!"

Everything about David frightened me. I was frightened of the razor blades sewn into his lapels. I was frightened by the way he would hit the quick-release buckle on his black leather belt—loaded with more razor blades and sharpened silver studs. I was frightened by the way he would grab it and swipe heads with it like he was preparing to rip open a face or two in some Teddy Boy fight.

"Just practising," Sean would say.

Before leaving for school that first morning, Mum and I knelt in front of the statue of Our Lady and said our full Rosary. Then, she kissed and hugged me, and I was gone.

Out.

I left Mum with a handkerchief comforting her face.

There was something different about that morning, and it was more than just missing Mass. I was someone else. Changed. Lighter, now that first layer of childhood had been stripped from me.

Some parents came on that first day. Some kids came with aunts and uncles who waited across the road after pushing threepenny bits or sixpences into the frightened kids' hands. Mum wanted to see me off, but I begged her not to. It would have ended in tears for the both of us. Strange, being so alone with so many other kids around me and who were probably feeling the same, but not one of us owning up to it.

Four double-decker buses were waiting near Manley Terrace. Mr. Hoban, Deputy Head, shouted us into order. Shuffling forwards in turn for the bus, I spotted Uncle David standing on the kerb, about a football pitch away, by the bowling green. It was his trench coat and funny hat that gave the game away.

I looked again. Gone.

16

PLAYGROUND BETS

David toured his brother Sean and I around the school. He was so big. So, too, were all of his friends. On that first day, everyone and everything seemed so huge; it was like walking in a land of giants.

Kitty's Diary

September 1959

Peter doesn't want other kids seeing me walking up the road with him. He's letting me stay the other side of the road.

Manley Terrace, where we were told to meet again that second morning, was bouncing with our school colours of grey and blue. A guy in sports gear hit our ears and jammed our mouths with his referee whistle. "Quiet!"

Kitty's Diary

Back home from seeing him off. Mrs. Marsden, Danny's mum, was not waving back.

Frightened didn't even come close.

"You *will* be quiet," shouted the sports gear. Silence jumped to a full stop. "Be sensible getting on the bus."

I didn't want to be 'sensible'. Street—you do *this*, or Street—you do *that*... I was one of the boys. Silence was happy.

Kitty's Diary

Thomas has, more than ever, been onto Peter about girls and drink. I've tried. Jesus, Mary, and Joseph, I've tried.

The school held about four hundred pupils through the yellow and blue windows that wrapped around the school. I could see one field and its goal post. There was a feeling of security about the place. I don't know why I felt that way. It was a new school and I was both frightened and excited. The third and fourth-years looked so big. The first few days, I stuck around with some boys from my junior school. Boys who weren't my friends. Boys who had often overpowered me.

We were brought into the main hall to meet the teachers, with their warm welcomes, introductions, and suggestions about surviving the next four years of school. We were no longer forced into long lines as we were in junior school, lines stinking of wet dog. We were no longer in a line of basin crops and crew cuts, our noses touching the back of someone's head. It felt great. We were all ready and silent, as the teachers stepped out from behind the stage curtain onto the four foot-high stage, looking down onto a hundred or so sparkling blue and grey school uniforms. None of the teachers looked angry. Somehow, they didn't seem as strict as the ones we had before. More relaxed. I recognised the sports and English teachers who had taught in our junior school. It was a different kind of fright than I had imagined. It was still scary, but somehow felt safer than junior school.

The playground was about kicking around a football. Teams of English Bulldogs were growing, and running into each other, while, close by, girls played two-ball. To the far right, a couple of fistfights were being thrown in for good measure. I was feeling different, more confident. Finally, with all that junior school trauma behind me, I felt like I wanted to be involved, but, at the same time, I didn't want to be.

I was back to being me: happy and okay being alone, but not lonely.

The playground was bouncing with the likes of others I'd never seen before, acknowledging each other with just a nod of the head, or a handshake, which was seen as being nice. It was noisy—*too* noisy. It was a new start for all of us, but more so for me. There were some really strange-looking kids, none more so than Dennis M with the black hair flopped down over half of his face. He was large and slow-looking, like it would be easy for anyone to take him for a ride. *Wrong*. He was razor sharp, and hard enough to cut through any crap thrown his way. Not only that, but he had three minders: his huge boxer-faced brothers who watched over him like a hawk. Dennis M welcomed and then challenged all the first years, regardless of size, to a bet. A 'certain winning' bet. I stood back and waited, watching lambs going to their slaughter, each waiting their turn in line. Dennis opened up his shirt to boast his naked chest, then bulged it out for anyone to hit as hard as they could. The bet invited first and second years to thump his chest and, if they could make him flinch or grimace, Dennis would lose the bet. It all sounded too easy.

The bet was that day's dinner money of two shillings against a one pound note, which his brothers held. He was like a street barker, voice bouncing against every wall, and sometimes also *through* the wall with, "Thump my chest as hard as you can!"

Why has he never asked ME? I was no bigger or tougher-looking than any of the other kids. I watched, open-mouthed, trying to work out what was happening.

"Stop shaking your head and thump my chest," he said to

one lad.

The boy lost his money.

Every so often, the smallest and weakest-looking boy would be dared by his friends to 'have a go'. Dennis wouldn't flinch. But there were the odd times when he would pretend to be hurt and shift back a few inches to help create more business. Every last one of those lambs lost that day's dinner money.

I stayed back to see how it all worked. Bets were placed on the coatroom floor below the coat racks, hidden from the teachers and goody-goody prefects. The two red-headed Parker brothers—big lads who boasted their second years— pushed through us. They were brothers from another school who were rumoured to have been expelled from every school they'd been in for bullying and fighting. They were with us at St. Anne's R.C. School after their parents had been forced into Bolton from the other side of Bury to a house just five minutes from our school. While the bet was being played out, Dennis' older twin and fourth-year brothers watched their young brother's back and gave the nod for the all-clear.

The baby-faced one of the two red-haired brothers bet a full ten-pack of Woodbines. Dennis M, cool as could be, snapped the pound note out to its full length and blew on it before placing it down on the foot bench. The two brothers rolled up their sleeves, the biggest spitting on his fist and smirking as he stepped forward. He turned to make sure everyone was going to watch him win. Confident, he leaned back as Dennis opened his shirt to prove nothing was protecting his bulged-out chest, then *whacked* it. The pounding didn't even make Dennis blink. Both brothers not only lost their cigarettes, but also their entire week's spending money. Dennis offered to sell the Woodbines back to them at a reduced rate, but they refused, storming off to bully some kid even weedier than me. Dennis butted in and, yes, there was some pushing and pulling between him and the red-haired brothers.

"Teacher!" someone shouted. Dennis smiled, turning his back on the teacher's pointing and wagging finger. Not so much the brothers, with their shocked, whiter-than-white faces.

Kitty's Diary
October 1959
He's hit the roof after Peter asked if just ONE pint of beer was okay.

A couple of days into half term, police were all over the place after rumours about the brothers from Bury regularly coming into school with bruised faces and busted lips. The taller of the two, who had supposedly kicked over some pub domino table, was walking with his leg in plaster after a couple of days in hospital. The brothers and the rest of their family had just vanished from the face of the earth.

In school, Dennis M continued with his bets.

Dennis jokingly asked if I wanted to bet, knowing I wouldn't accept. I backed away, but he could see I wasn't frightened of him or his hard-looking brothers. I stayed there, behind the jackets, where guys of all shapes and sizes would try their luck. Regardless of how they tried to make their fist firmer by hiding something solid in the palm of their hands, Dennis *always* won. Later, he would go around the school selling whatever he could, cutting his price well below the tuck shop. The tuck shop people came into the school complaining to Mr. Byrnes, the headmaster, about losing customers. "We can't stop something we can't see," the head told them. "You've seen the posters and warnings about this practice. But unless someone comes forward, or we catch someone in the act, there's nothing we can do."

Regardless of how many times the tuck shop owner complained, Dennis M was never found out. The tuck shop closed about eighteen months later. Dennis M kept the prices low, but charged extra for those wanting to gamble at thumping his chest.

17

CLASS C

Kitty's Diary

March 1961

He won't let Peter go to school on his bike. 'Too dangerous for a young boy'. Six-mile round trip—not too dangerous!

At school, some boys tried to get the better of Dennis M, with threats of older brothers or parents coming to 'get' him once school was out, but Dennis, in his usual unfazed way, would just say, 'I know where you live'. Their gamble lost them everything. After his wins, and alone, Dennis beckoned me from my everyday hiding place in the coatroom. "Fancy a free go?" I never found out why I was being treated to such a privilege. His chest bulged out as he told me to hit it as hard as I could. He nodded, stood firm, and then, with all my strength, I whacked him in exactly the place he had pointed to. Holding his chest, he fell back. I didn't feel like whooping or teasing him about being beaten. Concerned, maybe a little frightened, I stepped forward. I bent over him and asked if he was okay. He stood up, smiling, "I've had teddy bears hit me harder."

All these years later, I still don't know why he gave me a free go and then pretended I'd hurt him. Even more puzzling was how he walked me over to his brothers who were bigger and even harder-looking than my now best friend Dennis, 'cock' of our school year. I didn't know, then, that I was going to see things I'd never seen before and meet guys and girls who would otherwise have never looked at me twice. Not only that, but I would be talking with them, too, which, before, would have been a complete no-no. Suddenly, I was one of their friends. Weird.

In 1968, Dennis M drowned in a canal while trying to rescue a dog.

Kitty's Diary

May 1961

Still can't get into his bloody bedroom.

Yellow door padlocked. Secrets.

I failed my first big school exam and was sent down to

Class C, third from bottom of the school year, where I was welcomed with open arms. It couldn't have been better. Well, I suppose it could have been. I could have passed for Class A. It was okay: I'd still have friends. Friends I thought should have been higher than Class C. They were the sort of lads who could reckon up the odds on horse racing, money won or lost: none were fazed, even by accumulators. They talked cars and motorbikes and places where they could buy second-hand bits. They talked car tax dodges, like using a dark brown label from a Guinness bottle, which was the same shape and colour of a tax disc. Lads who would later follow their dads and brothers into demolition or the fairgrounds.

They'd boast how their fathers sometimes earned more than our teachers. How they knew that, I never found out. A couple of them talked about their fathers being steel erectors, which was always cash in hand, though they looked like they didn't own a penny between them. While I found it strange, it also seemed so natural. It sort of reminded me of Dad's wheeling and dealings, which made me wonder if they knew Dad, and thought I was somehow one of them. It seemed so strange being accepted without question into their group without them really knowing who I was.

They often talked about their uncles, brothers and fathers who were daring steel men working hundreds of feet up, running along the foot-wide iron girders while carrying heavy tools, as though they were on the ground. And again, strange how they would only boast between themselves about earning wedges of pound notes—enough to choke a donkey. Dad once told me about such people: how they were in a class of their own, families moving in and out of society when it suited them. They were not travellers, Irish tinkers, or Roma—just hard workers and hard drinkers who no one really knew anything about.

None of them ever asked anything about me and trusted me not to give away any of their secrets. I promised I wouldn't, and I never did. They didn't laugh when I asked if they could smell some of the same things which hit my nose; if I didn't talk, they never asked what was wrong. It was strange: being with those who were on the margins of society, I never felt I needed to escape. They were like me, but in a very different way. It all began to make sense when one of their fathers, who I had not met before, asked how Dad was. Their families invited me to join them. They would all start hitting the booze and, once, someone offered me a drink, but the man who knew Dad shouted, "No, Peter doesn't drink."

Kitty's Diary
Peter seems happy.

Second Year

My following year was a learning year: mostly non-school

learning from the other boys my age. I was making more friends and doing gymnastics. I was good on the wooden horse, climbing the ropes, and doing forward rolls on the mats. Yet, I was a complete failure in most things in the classroom. I tried, *really* tried to make friends with my education but we couldn't get it together: we just didn't understand each other. Technical drawing, with straight lines crossing other straight lines, hurt my thinking. I couldn't do it. It was the same with wood and metalwork: none of those subjects liked me.

Mr. Booth, our nice metalwork teacher, asked us to think of something to make. The other kids talked of pokers for the fire. When my brain fell out and smashed onto the ground, one of the boys asked, "Why are you staring at the floor?" He would have thought me potty if I had told him. I needed to get away from metalwork and from the other guys with their pokers and door handles, boasting all their achievements. I couldn't do it and my lack of understanding was hurting me. Mr. Booth placed a wire brush in my hand and told me to rub down some pokers the previous class had made.

I tried to get on with metalwork, but we just weren't suited. I even tried looking the part in my homemade apron, which stayed whiter than white and whose fancy invisible stitching was complimented by the art teacher. Mum had taught me dress-making skills on those boring wet days, when 'only children feel it's a dead day'.

There were others in the same mind, though, like Dennis M, who just knew how to work out racehorse and greyhound racing bets. While he somehow knew and understood numbers, he was oddly hopeless at everything else. For the first time, I was not alone, and that made me feel good. My confidence grew higher than I could have ever imagined and, with it, came a newfound freedom.

Kitty's Diary

December 1961

He still won't talk about his bloody yellow door. Not even why it's yellow!

It was Dad who suggested I talk with the headmaster about my difficulties with the 'boy' subjects. "You're good at baking, so why don't you ask if you could go into the cooking class?" Within a week, I carried a basket like the girls. I thought I'd be made fun of. No. Dennis made sure of that. Just him being close to me prevented anyone from making fun or stealing my freshly baked bread or cakes. Those weeks and months, every double lesson was baking, and, for me, it was my dream world. I had found myself in bread, cakes, and fruit pies. Best of all, I made our Christmas cake that year. Dad clapped when I placed it on the table.

18

RACHEL'S RETURN

May 1962

I was in the back street during a school holiday, having a
kickabout with my favourite ball and wall, when...

"Hello."

"Rachel!" We hugged and she asked what I had been up
to while she'd been away. She apologised for not being able
to stay long: it was just a short visit. But I really needed to
talk about school and how Dad thought girls wouldn't be
good for a young boy like me. There was a short silence. She
looked sad, disappointed. I hadn't seen her like that before.

"What's wrong?"

She smiled a forced smile and then walked off.

"Wait for me," I said, following after her.

She stopped at the corner of Blackburn Road, "Well, hurry up, then."

We sneaked out, careful not to let Dad see us, and took a shortcut through Astley Bridge cemetery. When we passed the 'dead church' on the hill, we heard some older voices reminiscing about the past, and we darted out of sight behind the big Romany gravestones. Rachel giggled as they laid flowers for their loved ones. We made a dash for it to our safe place behind the bowling shed, where we rested among the sweet, fruit-scented flowers in the shade of a huge pink rhododendron. We talked school and parents. We talked about wishing for a sibling. We talked loneliness. We shared secrets. We chatted about the last two years and I even asked her all my questions about sex and what all those words meant. She didn't laugh or make fun of my naivety. She explained everything, even about periods. All things Mum and Dad thought I shouldn't know. She kissed my cheek and then gave me a quick peck on the lips. I pulled back. I hadn't meant to. It was just a surprise. I said sorry and kissed her back. I really loved her; I had done from the very beginning. There was something about her, which, even now after all these years, I can't explain.

I cried and told her how much I missed her. She knew why. "Take no notice of your Dad. It's him who has the problem." There had never been silence between us before.

"I know," I said, finally. She asked about Dad's secret

rooms. "Still secret."

We shared so many things, and yet she gave no clue as to where she'd been for the last couple of years, and if it was even the same country. Where had her usual vanishing act taken her? I didn't understand. She said, "I missed you, too." She wouldn't explain why there were never any postcards or letters. There was another long silence. My constant questioning seemed to annoy her, so I gave up.

"And is your mum still a slave?" I had never heard her use the word 'slave' before.

"What do you mean?"

"The way he doesn't use the ashtray. Just flicking his ash on the carpet like that. And she runs around brushing it all up."

I tried telling her it wasn't like that anymore, with the Hoover vacuum and posh washing machine. I told her about everything he'd done for us. I thought she would be pleased, but no; she seemed angry, just shrugging her shoulders. Deep down, I knew she was right. She had always been honest and truthful. Even Mum would talk about him not being the same man. So, who *was* he?

I pushed her again to tell me where she had been, and it pushed her to the wire. "Why is your face so red?" I said. "You look like you're going to explode." Nothing. Just more secrets. Always secrets.

Then, suddenly, she blurted, "Does he still think I'll give

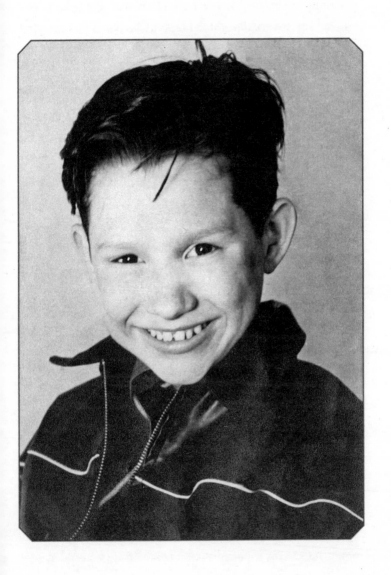

you some disease?" Before I could answer, she got up and hurried away. I tried to catch her, but she was a fast runner.

***

A couple of days later, Rachel and her mum had already vanished again, so I got it back together with my ball and the wall. I had left my very best friends behind while Rachel and I walked and talked, me wittering on as though I was deaf to her news about the boys she'd dated. I would never forget that meeting, despite those few minutes we'd had words. I would soon miss every word and every moment with her. I'd even miss the way she swept back her hair and how it would flop onto her face as though it liked to be flicked. I felt a tightness in my chest, fearing I would never see her again. I wished and wished that I was wrong. I was so desperate to see her again. I even said my Rosary, and after school would go looking for her. But she and her mum really had gone, to wherever it was they always went.

Thirteen, and I was seeing girls differently. I was looking at their breasts, bottoms, and the way they moved. I observed how the older boys would ask them out on dates. I watched them drink beer—it didn't seem to change them in any way, like Dad said it would. A few underage lads boasted about going into pubs, especially the ones who looked older, like

Paul Wilson. He was over six feet at just fifteen. I hadn't really understood what Dad meant about girls and boys changing, or when the older boys talked about their girlfriends being 'on the rag'. I didn't understand anything about anything. I didn't even understand why Dad said I wasn't to sit on the toilet boards.

There was something different about everything and it was confusing. I wished for a girlfriend, but, at the same time, I was glad I didn't have one. I've only ever liked being touched by those I can trust. Both the boys and the girls bashed my ears; that, or I filled theirs with silence.

Everything was wrong. They were wrong. My world was wrong.

I confessed to my priest that I was having dreams about girls. "Say five Hail Marys and six Our Fathers." His tone changed. "You are still sleeping with your arms across your chest, as the teacher told you?" There was a long silence as I recalled the teacher's words: 'If you die in the night and your arms are not crossed, you won't go to Heaven'. I didn't wait for my blessing. I stood up and walked out.

I went back to my wall, my football, and my bike.

Despite everything, life was better because of Rachel.

19

COMING THE DREAM

October 1962

There was an ear-bashing silence in the school playground as two fourth-years from different schools stood with just a couple of yards holding them apart. Hands in front of their waists, ready to snap the quick release of the buckles of their studded, razor blade belts. They circled slowly round, anticipating each other's movements in a deafening silence before buckles slapped and their belts dropped into their hands. The bigger guy with a quiff kicked out but missed, then the smaller one wearing the red coat whipped his belt, just missing the other's face. I wanted it to stop, yet I wanted it to carry on so I could see the blood and watch them run for stitches. I'd never seen blood rip open a face before. The crowd was excited and frightened in equal amounts. Gasps as blood and skin flew across the yard and splattered the concrete. Police cars screaming towards us. Studded belts still whipping, and bloody bits flying all over the place. The sounds of teachers and police, and everyone running away. I was in a blizzard of people bashing me from all sides. Panic was running through my bones, freezing me to the spot. Alone, I felt free. My head escaped; my breathing eased.

***

Back home, after tea, the wall and I got it together. We were a better team than Batman and Robin. We were just so good together, knocking the ball back to each other as we did. Mum and Dad kept coming out asking if I was okay playing on my own. I wanted to tell them about my best friends, but they wouldn't have listened. Many times, Mum would ask why I was no good at keeping friends. Maybe that's why she hated my wall, because we were so good together. She never understood. She tried her best, but she saw other kids enjoying the craic. The wall and I didn't want anyone else messing up our game, though. Every so often, some part-time mates would come round asking to play. The wall and I enjoyed that bit of a change, but within days they would leave, only returning weeks, sometimes months later for another game.

***

School sports day, I was chosen for the football team. It seemed natural, volunteering to go into the net. Mr. Brent, after I'd saved some difficult shots, said I was a natural. That first game helped me get the school goalkeeper's jumper. When I told Dad, he started to cry. Between sobs, "It's something I wanted to do, but the war put a stop to that."

He never explained why he suddenly changed the conversation from my football to World War I. He talked of his time at training camp, where his best friend accidentally blew himself up with a hand grenade, and how someone shot themselves in the foot. He talked of biscuits so hard they had to be dipped in tea to soften them, and blocks of chocolate so hard and so big they would knock you out if they hit you in the face. He banged a Woodbine, then finally returned to my football. He seemed to know my ambition was to become a footballer. Then, again, he suddenly took over and started talking about Stanley Mathews, and also Dick Pym, who was in goal for Bolton Wanderers. I never found out how he knew all about Russian goalkeeper Lev Yashin. Dad loved sport. All sport. He talked about heavyweight boxing champion Jack Johnson, too, and started throwing punches at imaginary fighters. I had never seen him ducking and diving like that before. He loved it. I loved it. He loved the idea of me going into sport and living his dream.

There was a short silence before I explained about my wall, and about my dreams. He was nodding to everything I was saying. He didn't move. He didn't even light up his Woodbine. His ears were wider than I had ever seen them, full of everything I was saying. He was with me for maybe an hour, a precious hour, my Dad. The Dad I never knew existed.

***

It was our first game in the school house teams. I volunteered for goalkeeper. Yes, I admit I missed the only ball that came my way. Crashed into the back of the net when Mr. Brent shouted, "Kelly, you got in the way of the keeper!"

The teachers seemed to be a little more at ease with me, all of a sudden acknowledging me in the corridors, congratulating me on my goalkeeping, "Peter, you did well in goal today!"

There was a new me happening and I was loving it. It was the same in class; no one really bothered me. I could sit at the back enjoying my daydreams. Okay, there was the rare occasion, like when the history teacher asked, "…and what date was that?" to which I responded with the actual day's date.

"It's Monday 10th, Miss." The whole class laughed, and I even caught the teacher grin. It felt good somehow. It didn't bother me, not being involved in the lesson; in fact,

I enjoyed it.

World Wars I and II were the subjects I knew most about. In history class I would talk endlessly about the film *All Quiet on the Western Front*. The teacher never stopped me. In fact, he encouraged it and my thoughts. Everything was going great, until one day, I blurted, "The Germans had it bad too. They may even have had it worse than the British." I explained how they had lacked food, clothes, shoes, everything, more so than the English. The soldiers too. No one was convinced. Kev Barrows was truly annoyed. He kept on shouting about his grandad's brothers who had died from the 'gas'. Teacher eased the atmosphere back before I carried on talking about the Germans.

Finally, sports teacher Mr. Brent walked in, and, in front of the whole class, threw me the green jumper and called, "Street, you are goalkeeper for our game against Brownlow Fold School. First round of the Bolton Wanderers Trophy and we have to win to reach the second round!" The class looked at me, at Mr. Brent, our history teacher, then back to me. There was only one attempted clap from Tony Broderick, but, noticing no one else join in, he stopped.

Kitty's Diary

November 1962

He keeps doing them weights. I keep telling him he's going to hurt himself 'down there', but he wants to build a body like Steve Reeves! He's seen all his films. He can try.

In the playground the next day, Tony Broderick came over. We chatted and he asked if I would like to be a Boy Scout. I had an idea what they were about. Seymour Road Scout group was only a ten-minute walk from my house. So... why *not*?

That Friday was my first Scouting day. Kids, aged eleven to sixteen, bouncing off the walls. It frightened me. The boss, scoutmaster Worsley, shouted, "Can we calm down, please?" It was freaky how they all just complied, no question. There were a few giggles and some pushing and shoving, but it quickly all went quiet without him having to say another word. I had not known what to expect, but there was no intimidation, which I imagined there might be.

For once in my young life, somehow, and for reasons I cannot explain, I felt at home. Safe. Scouting was going to be for me.

***

One morning, having lifted my heaviest weights yet at the gym the night before, I woke with something pink oozing out of my belly button. Mum's warning about 'doing some damage down there' was banging my ears. I hurried off to Dr. John's surgery. I didn't mind that I had to wait almost an hour—I just hoped he wouldn't tell Mum about my hurting myself.

The big guy was sitting at the side of his desk when I walked in. Nervous, I told him I'd done something 'down there'. I pleaded him not to tell Mum. In his Scottish accent, he told me to lie on the couch and lift my top. He looked at the problem, then looked at me, shook his head, and, with his long thumbnail, picked out the pink stuff. Trying his best to keep a straight face, he said, "Don't go to bed with gum in your mouth."

That night, Dad came home early after hearing from one of the other dads whose boy was in the same class as me. Never once had Dad ever left work early, not even when he heard about his brother dying. He took off his overalls, washed his arms and hands free of all signs of coal, then handed me ten shillings for a 'celebration meal'.

Three portions of fish and chips, followed by a tub of Neapolitan ice cream. I was tingling with excitement. After our meal, my ball and I were ready for our moment with the wall. That's when Dad suddenly burst into tears. When I asked Mum, she explained that they were 'happy tears' because he was so proud. His son was going to play football as he himself had wanted—had it not been for the wars. The idea of me playing in goal for the school team was something he never thought would happen. Neither did I, really. And it was all down to the wall.

20

TONY AND SCOUTING

I was out the back, warming up for a great game between Man United and Real Madrid. I was Real Madrid. Then, Tony Broderick came round and asked to join in. Our woollen jumpers and jackets were laid down, a foot from the wall. This was getting better and better. Soon, we were having a kickabout with the wall and, before I knew it, there was Mick Hargreaves, too, big Neil Bradshaw, and enough friends for a five-a-side game. I was in heaven. Heaven with all the shouting: "Pass it over!", "Great shot", "Goal!"

For an hour or so, everything was going great. Then, all of a sudden, a sickly tight feeling in my chest. I had to break away from them. I couldn't help it. Jumpers were picked up as Mick Hargreaves shouted something about going to the park. I wanted, *really* wanted, to go with them. But my chest, and part of my head, held me back. They never came round again. It was both upsetting and joyous—I wasn't sure how those two emotions came together. I seemed to make friends so easily, but just couldn't manage to keep them.

For the next six weeks, I shared more time with my wall and the toilet. Alone, but not lonely. I would never understand how I could spend so much time on my own and yet be happy. Others would complain, some even cried, about being on their own, feeling somehow unwanted or betrayed. There was something wrong with them. Why would they want to be with someone other than themselves *all* the time? They even went sleeping at each other's houses for company if parents were away or something. It all seemed so strange to me.

***

I was getting ready to leave for school one day when Dad returned after heading off to work, shouting something about his marlin spike which he used for splicing the ropes. I'd never seen him in such a hurry, freaking about having a bad day. He raced up the stairs and unlocked his yellow door. When he came back out, he paused a few seconds, as he always did before locking that door to check and double-check it was secure. But this time, it didn't happen. He must have forgotten in his hurry, racing back down, still shouting about snapping ropes.

This was my moment. Finally, after thirteen years, I was going to find the secret in there that Mum and I had never been allowed to see. I still don't know why I crept up the stairs like I did. I could have easily run up; the noise didn't matter any longer. I hadn't noticed before just how big and heavy the door handle was. My mind was so taken from me, concentrating so hard on that door, that I didn't hear trouble stomping up the stairs.

"Keep out—that's *my* room." I'd never seen Dad so angry. His face and neck were bursting into flames. He pulled out his bunch of keys and, before locking the door, pushed me so hard to one side I hit the landing wall.

Over the evening's meal of hotpot, nothing was said about his yellow door.

Scout Night

My new friend, Tony, suggested I follow him to the Scout group and speak with Mr Worsley and his assistant Mr Higgins. Their first question was, "Are you a relation of Thomas Street?" I nodded. "Well, give your Dad the very best, and tell him, the drains are still perfect."

That was it. Nothing else said. I was in. I was a Boy Scout with the twentieth Bolton Seymour Road Scout Group. It was also a Scout band which would lead all the other local Scout groups around Bolton on St. George's Day. Suddenly, without realising it, I had become part of a large non-Catholic family. I went home and told Mum. She was kind of okay with it, but suggested I still go and inform my priest. She warned me that he would probably tell me to carry my rosary and catechism everywhere, especially when I was around my newfound Protestant friends. "And while you're there, ask him to bless the St. Christopher medal I bought for you."

Later, just before Dad came in from work, I found Mum in the front room crying. She wouldn't tell me what was wrong or show me the letter she'd let drop to the floor. The envelope was in Grandma's writing. Mum picked it up and stuffed it in her pocket. I saw Dad reading that very same letter when he got home. He read it over and over. They started talking, and Dad placed his arm around her, letting her cry it out. It was the first time I saw physical contact between them. I asked and asked about the letter, but it was always the same, "It's just a letter from your Grandma." More letters came from Grandma and with each one, more tears flooded our front room.

Friday night was Scouting night. We chalked a compass on the floor, and everything was great, until I realised that I couldn't tell which was north, south, east or west. The other boys were loving it, and even began splitting the compass into smaller parts like south-south-west, and even more than that. None of it was working for me, yet they didn't tease me about it. Half a dozen times, the compass was wiped clean, then re-chalked. After the other boys had completed the compass test, EAST had changed places with NORTH, SOUTH with WEST, each part of the compass staring up at me.

In the evening, we lit a small fire using just two matches and no paper. Life was great. Okay, on rainy Scout nights we would play 'British Bulldog', the rough, tag game I never liked for fear of getting hurt and not being able to play football. But life was good.

Kitty's Diary
November 1962

Peter's been telling the priest about his new Scouting friends. He knows he won't set on fire if he hangs around with the non-Catholic kids.

21

BECKY AND THE FIFE

I was getting more and more confident going places with kids from school and their friends. Every Saturday, we would meet in Sammie's Cafe, a pale copy of an American milk bar, a couple of hundred yards down from the Iron Church on Blackburn Road. My clone was there in the middle of ten, maybe fifteen, friends, listening to Elvis and The Beatles while drinking colas, frothy coffees, and milk shakes. We would be laughing and joking, and I would be acting around, while my *real* me was further down the cafe, watching everyone.

It was Becky, between sips of cola, who started talking about Robert Mitchum in *Heaven Knows, Mr. Allison*, and commenting on the actor's good looks. She talked and talked about him. Once home, thinking about Becky and her thoughts of Mitchum, I sneaked a couple of Dad's cigs, and tried smoking from the side of my mouth. Within a minute, I felt dizzy and wanted to vomit. I fell asleep pinching my chin while saying my prayers, hoping I would wake with a double chin, just like Mitchum's. In the morning I checked the mirror. Nothing had changed. After that I gave up trying to look like him.

Becky was almost three years older than me. She was the one who had taught me how to play two-ball against my brick wall. We were good friends, and, like Rachel, I used to plait her hair and be her face model when she wanted to try out different coloured lipsticks. That had been a few years before and I'd not seen her since, so that Saturday when she walked into Sammie's, with those skin-tight jeans and bra strap just peeking out from her white blouse, it sent my imagination into overdrive. Becky was everywhere. She'd been in my dreams and was still in my head when I woke in the morning. She was with me in class and in the back street. I needed to kiss her. I would go into my bedroom and practise my kissing technique on the back of my hand while holding a pillow, like John Wayne with Maureen O'Hara in *The Quiet Man*.

It was a couple of weeks later when I was sharing my wall with a Saturday morning that she saw me there, alone. She smiled and came over; I let my football drift off somewhere.

It was the way she leaned back against the wall, forcing my thoughts to take over my mouth, "Can I kiss you?"

She smiled, nodded.

This was it. This was my moment. I stepped closer. She winced when I stood on her toes and my teeth clashed with hers. I was ready to hide inside myself when she put her arms around me and kissed me back. Such a long kiss. I was on the verge of happy tears. She held me like I had never been held before.

After that, her soft floral Tweed perfume was all over my thoughts as my tongue traced my lips over and over, tasting her breath and sweet lipstick.

Some things one *never* forgets.

That weekend, I went to tell my priest about the new girls I was dreaming about. He was very loud when he exclaimed, "Stop dreaming about girls. It's not good for a boy of your age! Ten Our Fathers and five Hail Marys."

Battered by all of those prayers, I knocked on the head any notion about visiting a non-Catholic church. Besides, I kept thinking how I'd never seen any of my Catholic mates combust after they'd been hanging around with non-Catholics. First chance I got, I scanned the church notice board. No sign of combustions. I didn't get it, there didn't seem to be any hang-ups from anyone about non-Catholics hanging around with Catholics. If I was going to combust, bring it on. I dared myself to hang around with non-Catholics.

Scout night, I was asked if I wanted to join the Scout band. Great! Scoutmaster Worsley gave me the choice of drums or fife. Of course, I was going to say drums, but then Broderick got there first. I always, always wanted to be in a band: I didn't know how, but it had happened. I was going to be a fife player. I would be one of eight others leading the Scout group. A fife player was, of course, far better than any drummer.

Fife

Mum didn't like my fife—she never explained why—but Dad *loved* it. He even encouraged me, but whenever he wanted me to play something, strange wind noises came out. Tuesday night was band practice night: 'When the Saints Go Marching In'. When the Scout leader unravelled the Union flag, fifes happened and drums followed. Fifes were up first, then the drums practised their bit. I was giving it my very best, and it sounded great to me. Silence blasted the room. Playing away, and unaware of everyone.

"You're out of tune," said David. "You're not playing any notes, you're just blowing." David, the grammar school boy, knew his fife back to front. He could even play the 'Z-Cars' theme.

All the drums were gawping at me. The fifes were grinning. My fingers became dizzy trying to find the holes. Those holes in the fife were teasing, somehow moving everywhere except where they should be. "What do you mean, it's not your fault? *Whose* fault is it?" They laughed. I answered it was fife's fault for moving the holes. I didn't think they were laughing at me. Teased, but accepted.

"You don't look too well," David said. "Looks like you've a cold coming on." I forced a cough.

"Don't come near us with that cold." I forced more coughs and then left with my pockets filled with their very best wishes.

Excuses helped keep me away from band practice. Some of my excuses were inspired, like helping circus people escort a camel into its compound on Queen's Park. Pure genius. Yes, there was a circus in town, so it was believable.

My fife and I didn't understand each other. I blew into it, and even moved my fingers up and down, as the other Scouts did. Whatever I did, the fife would only blow out a single note—the very same note—every time it went to play. I decided I would stop trying. Instead, I would pretend to play and just hope no one would notice, with the drums showing off and giving it their very best.

A couple of weekends later, on Saint George's Day, our drums and fifes, with flags waving to everyone, escorted the Great Lever Scout Group up Swan Lane, along Lever Edge Lane, and then down to St. Bede's C of E church. It wasn't the best of weather, so I told the other Scouts, including the Scoutmaster, that if I went into that church I could burst into flames. Yes, there were giggles and a few funny looks, but then Kenny Mathews explained it was a Catholic thing with 'Proddie' churches and that I could end up in limbo.

They all stepped into line, soldier-like, and walked in perfect time to a single, slow drumbeat. I watched them all walk off and into St. Bede's as I waited outside, relieved at not having been forced into the church, just in case I *did* burst into flames. It was a freezing cold morning. I was leaning back against the wall of a red brick house with a nice garden behind the church, when an elderly couple from the house beckoned and asked if I wanted to wait inside. Their breakfast smells dragged my nose into the back room, where plates shared bacon and eggs with the man and his wife. I think the woman must have seen that the bacon was teasing my nose. "Would you like a bacon sandwich?" she asked.

"Please."

"You play the fife?"

"I just got it this morning," I lied. A bacon butty, with brown sauce, snuffed out more questions. Questions about my fife and what I could play.

"Before the war, I was a bugle boy in the Boy's Brigade," said the man.

His wife gave him a funny look. "You've never mentioned that before."

"Well, I *was*."

I muttered that I couldn't play and just held the fife up to my mouth, which they accepted.

22

JENNIFER, MISS BRETHERTON, AND THE BOLTON BOYS

1st December 1962

Seymour Road Youth Club. Bobby Darin playing. Jennifer's black hair and blue eyes took my breath away. A love ache was squeezing my chest, so I had to ask her for a date. Her friend, Carole Mather, all excited, came over giggling, "Jennifer would like to know if you'd go out with her." I walked away without saying a word, anger and ignorance shouting at me.

Kitty's Diary

December 1962

He'll not tell Peter about girls. He didn't think I would shout at him like that.

I rested on the low wall on Blackburn Road and cried. I couldn't understand what was happening. There was something different about me. The past six weeks I had spent with Jennifer were the best I had ever known. Life was just wonderful until Dad's warnings took over my brain, and I almost dropped her from my life, but, once his ideas had finally drained from my head, I started seeing her again.

Yes, I was allowed the odd squeeze of her breast, but that was as far as it went. Dad would never tell me who had grassed on us, but, somehow, he found out about us walking together through Bluebell Woods. The stress of it all became too much. It was Jennifer who broke it off in the end, and she cried, even though she didn't want to see me again. She yelled about someone going round to her house and saying I'd taken her down into the old woods. It was all so strange. Secrets. All the time there were secrets. We bumped into each other again five years later. There were no words. Not even a smile. Just a gentle nod from me to her, and she to me. Even now I still think of her, and *what if?*

***

Life was beginning to happen again, starting with Miss Bretherton, our music teacher. I couldn't understand anything about 'crotchets', 'quavers', or 'minims', but I *could* understand her blonde hair, slim figure, and those

American tan nylon stockings she wore. Not only that, but once, when she crossed her legs, I peeked the top of those nylon stockings. She was probably the most beautiful woman I had ever seen. Even more beautiful than Vivienne Leigh. Every day I would slick my hair with Brylcreem into an Elvis-like quiff.

I was always dreaming about her. She was everything. Everywhere. Everyone was Miss Bretherton. At every opportunity, I would walk past her house on Blackburn Road. I would stop and pretend to look through the antique shop window next door.

One day, on my way home from the park after playing football, muddied, hair all over the place, I was passing by her house when she stepped out. "It's Peter, isn't it?"

My mouth refused to move. Shut tight. My brain was telling me to speak. Telling me to say how much I loved her. Finally, I came out with, "Hello, Miss Bretherton." It was all my mouth would allow.

The following term, it was announced that Miss Bretherton, newly married, was moving to Australia with her husband. I must have been the only one who didn't clap. My wall and I were back spending more time with each other. Being chosen for the school team made it more important than ever to keep up my confidence. I chalked goalposts on the wall, then, standing further and further back, I would throw the ball to marked spots on its red body. High-up balls were sent

Scout Band

Bolton Boys

back, as though I was catching corner kicks. Football was replacing Miss Bretherton.

Life really returned when I was asked to be goalkeeper for the school. I grew at least ten feet when Mr. Brent came into class, throwing the school goalkeeper kit and shouting, "Street, you're in goal again! Keep this up," he added, "and you'll be playing for Bolton Boys, Lancashire, and maybe England under-fifteens."

There was something different about being in goal; it seemed the perfect position for me to be in. I wasn't one of the pack, chasing the ball around. I was alone, but not lonely. I was separate from everyone. For the first time in my life, I was somebody. I stood out. Before being chosen for goalkeeper, I had been invisible to everyone, including the teachers, but now, people wanted to know me. Everyone asked about my goalkeeping skills and how I had become so good at it. It was strange. It seemed as though the ones who were clever at everything except football had now become invisible.

Kitty's Diary

March 1963

He caught me trying his yellow door. All these years he's kept me out. What is it about that bloody room? His dirty laundry—freshly washed, ironed, and left on the landing. Bloody yellow door.

I was goalkeeper for our St. Anne's school team, keeping a clean goal most of the time. I ran the two miles back home to tell Dad there was a chance of me playing Burnden Park in the Bolton Wanderers under-fifteens cup final. Not only that, but playing on Burnden Park would mean I'd be in the nets where Eddie Hopkinson kept many a clean sheet for Bolton and England. I don't know what happened, but when I told him, he started to cry. I was so excited, I bounced off every wall of 339 Blackburn Road. Dad was still crying. He cried more or less all night. Mum said it was because he was so proud, but I sensed it was more than that.

Mr. Bridill, our new maths teacher and ex-Borstal teacher, ruled the class with a rod of iron. When Tony wouldn't stop singing 'Love me Do', Mr. Bridill kicked his desk *so* hard it smashed into his groin. He cried for the first half of the lesson. Mr. Bridill refused his request to leave the room, "That's what you get when you mess with *me*."

Break time, I stood well away from everyone, in my own world, when Mr. Bridill, for the first time, came over, nodded, then stunned me by commenting I had an important game that Saturday. "It's the Hill School." He saw my surprise. "Mr. Brent said you have a big game this Saturday: semi-final for the cup. Isn't that right?" He knew everything about it. He even knew the name David Leyton, a superb main player on the other team and the hard fighter 'cock' of the school. I heard Mr. Bridill's intake of air before he nodded and added, "You can win this. Just keep your mind on the game." Before leaving to sort out a fight, he patted me on the shoulder and wished me luck, saying he couldn't make the game, but he would be thinking of me. "Mr. Brent thinks you are good enough for the England under-fifteens and maybe even professional in a few years' time." He smiled then moved away. I really had wanted to say something in response. Whenever it was his turn to supervise the school yard, he would come over and we would talk Bolton Wanderers.

Kitty's Diary
April 1963
Hopkinson, Hopkinson. That's ALL Peter talks about.

Everyone had been talking about it. Other teachers who had never spoken to me before came to wish me luck for the game.

Saturday. The day could not have been better for me, with a bit of rain the night before, making the goal mouth just right for diving. The opposing team were onto the pitch first. Then, there he was, looking me up and down, while the rest of our team gawped at his five foot eight of solid muscle and mop of black hair. My centre-half and back knew their job that day was to stop Leyton getting through. It was one-nil to us with just five minutes to go, when the charging bull finally broke through: he was chasing to get the ball passed to him from the left wing. He was almost with the ball when my legs and whole being headed and dived at his feet and caught the loose ball, seconds before he would have banged the ball into the net. Going too fast to stop, he almost collided into me, but leapt over in an effort to avoid it. I had winded myself with the dive. He turned back to see if I was okay, nodded, then helped me back up onto my feet. Final whistle, with a one-nil to us.

Yes, there was a sudden flare in my life, yet I was still separate from everyone. I wanted all the fuss, but I didn't, because it somehow felt awkward, and came with a slight overpowering feeling in my chest. A change was about to happen that I wasn't sure I was ready for. I could handle it, I thought, but only in small, controlled doses.

Everyone who knew the opposing team had almost convinced us we were the underdogs to Smithill's—top of the Lancashire school footy teams. They had played and won against all the best school teams in the North West. Not only that, but they had won the cup *every* time. There had been talk around the school and Astley Bridge Park about us losing ten-nil. Everyone knew I had played for the Mid Lancs team. I was the only one in the team who had played with such strong, talented guys. The pressure was on me to stop anything and everything coming my way. I could hear people talking behind my back and I was loving *every* minute. Suddenly, I was visible to everyone. Could I handle it? Yes, I could, and I *did* handle it. Most probably doubted me, but I could feel my confidence and excellence growing, almost to the point of exploding. All the teachers were talking to me. Even those teachers from the top classes, who had never spoken to me before, were stopping me in the corridor and asking for my thoughts and how I felt about beating such a strong team like Smithill's.

My whole life was changing. In those two weeks leading up to the big game, everyone around the neighbourhood was talking to me. Not only that, but I was being congratulated and wished well for the big game. The sports teacher gave us fifty tickets for our game on Burden Park, to sell. We sold out. Dennis M came over and took odds on us winning. The odds were not looking good for us, though. Dennis said something about being down 4-1. There was a buzz around the school. Stella Hargreaves, the most beautiful girl in the school, came up to me at dinner time, with everyone watching, and gave me a long, seductive kiss on the lips.

There was talk of me trialling for the under-sixteen England team, and, from there, it would be a trial for a league club. I began to dream what it would be like to be a professional goalkeeper.

Life was good.

23

BURNDEN PARK

'St. Anne's goalkeeper, Street, makes a fine save,
punching the ball clear in the final of the Bolton
Wanderers Cup at Burnden Park, last night.'
Bolton Evening News, Wednesday 1st May 1963

All kitted up in the famous Wanderers changing room,
and Mr. Brent walked in. "Look, you have nothing to
lose. They're the ones who'll be under pressure: *they* have
everything to lose. You can do this!"

It was then that manager, Bill Ridding, walked in and
shook us all by the hand, then looked over at me. "Weren't
you in goal for Bolton Boys?" He didn't wait for an answer.
"I saw you in the line-up on Bromwich Street." There was a
slight pause before he wished us all the very best.

● From a short centre from County Secondary Technical School outside right Collier, St. Anne's R C School goalkeeper Street makes a fine save, punching the ball clear in the final of the Bolton Wanderers' Cup at Burnden Park last night. The match was drawn 3-3.

SWAILES HAT-TRICK EARNS CUP REPLAY

AFTER starting firm favourites to retain Bolton Schools' Athletic Association's Bolton Wanderers' Cup, C S Technical School boys were happy to secure a 3-3 draw against St. Anne's R C S at Burnden Park last night. Both teams displayed a forceful type of football, but the honours went to St. Anne's boys, who three times fought back to draw level when defeat seemed certain.

That was it. Simple. There are some things you never forget and one of them was Mr. Brent's talk that day. One of my unforgettable moments. We were all ready, and just yards from the incredibly famous Bolton Wanderers footy pitch. There, waiting for both teams, was the tunnel that some of the world's greatest footballers had passed through onto the pitch. There must have been around four hundred lions in the stands, all roaring at the same time for their team. Then, a sudden gag of the lions as we went into our positions. I looked into the crowd for Dad and was sure I saw him in the front, standing on his seat, fingers to his mouth, whistling. I savoured every footstep, every intake of breath, as I walked toward the nets. I had dreamt about that moment so many times and suddenly there I was. Once on my goal line, I touched each goal post and jumped to touch the crossbar. This was me. This was going to be my place. *My* nets in years to come.

All the people we knew, and more besides, were in the stands. The very same stands Dad had brought me to see Bolton versus Wolves in the cup match. Manchester United were there and many others I didn't know, seated in the same row as Mum and Dad. None of us had ever walked into a space before where we would be eaten alive in front of a good few thousand men, women, and children. I could see their mouths shouting and their flags and rattles moving, but, for some reason, I couldn't hear a sound. In my mind's eye,

I could see Dad running his tongue to and fro, the way he always did. Then, when the ref blew the kick-off whistle, everyone apart from us all just suddenly disappeared. There was an excitement I had never experienced before. I was on the same football ground and in the same goal as Hopkinson, all thanks to my wall, who had been training me to dive, catch the ball, and leap into the air to punch the ball away. It would all come back, like second nature.

Smithill's were coming at us like a tour de force, regardless of how much Chris, John, and Gary—my back three—battled to stop their forwards coming at me. Ball after ball was coming in. I low-dived and fingertipped the ball around the goal posts, just like Eddie. I was doing high saves, low saves. I was running for the ball which had been hit just too far, when the other side's centre forward stretched with everything he had, but it wasn't enough: I dived in and saved the ball. Then there was that one which came into the top right. I missed. 1-0 to them. I had to keep it together, knowing there would be football scouts watching me, just as Mr. Brent had talked about.

I don't know what Alf, our captain, said to the team, but suddenly things turned, and a new life came about them. No one was greedy with the ball; it was being passed from one player to the next. There was a move forward, fast: it was Alf who had timed it perfectly to come in, leaving their back line in disarray, and he took the ball. The goalkeeper didn't stand a chance: 1-1. Now I was kicking the ball almost to the halfway line. That was when the shot came in and my hand, without me knowing, tipped it over the bar.

Half time. We were given segments of orange and a sip of water to drink. Mr. Brent talked tactics with the players, then turned back to me. "You are the last one who can save us." It took my breath away. The trust in that moment was more than I had ever received. "Don't give them a chance. As soon as the ball gets anywhere near, you go for it. Grab it—don't be afraid. He'll have to jump over you!"

We were the first to score, and the second goal, too. Then they came roaring back, equalling: 2-2. I was out of position when a high ball came in and blasted the back of my net: 3-2. Ten minutes to go when our captain, Alf, somehow managed to weave in and out before hitting the ball into the top right-hand corner: 3-3. Eight minutes to go. The lions came at us. We were really prepared for them: we'd heard how ruthless they could be, but nothing like the power and agility they were coming at us with. Steve, the forward who had tried out for United, came charging. He blasted the ball low to my left. I dived and tipped it round the post. It was their corner which came in high, and I leapt up, punching the ball as hard as I could. My John, centre back, took it forward just as the whistle blew full time.

All our instincts, all eleven of us, kicked in and, somehow, we kept the score 3-3, and won the replay by 4-1. Mr. Brent said he was going to put my name forward to try out for the England under-fifteens team. In that moment I recalled his words, 'Practise, practise, practise'. The other guys in the team were relishing being hugged and crowded around, but something wasn't right about it for me. I wasn't enjoying it and I didn't want any of it to be happening. Yes, a few pats on the back were okay with me—even a hug—but not being crowded like that.

***

Back at school, myself and the rest of the team were called up on stage to receive our football medals. The whole school was clapping. This was me. This was how it was going to be for the rest of my life. I was going to be a professional goalkeeper.

Back home, I chalked a goal post on the wall, ready for a kickabout. We were still so good together. It watched me throw high balls and knocked them back, higher than ever. My goalkeeping skills were getting even better. Then, another unforgettable moment: seeing Rachel come round that corner. She wasn't the same Rachel, though. Her dark hair was no longer short, but now flowing over her shoulders. Gone were the tight jeans, replaced with a skirt that fell just below her knees, and instead of the dark shirt and denim jacket—a brightly coloured blouse peeking through a soft wool jumper. Her trainers had gone, too, in favour of some flat leather pumps and bobby socks.

We hugged. I couldn't speak. Like always, she had just turned up out of the blue, like magic. I recognised her silence. "We're going to live in Holland," she said, between her tears. We hugged and cried together. This time was certain to be the last time we would see each other and share our secrets. Blackburn Road took fifteen minutes to walk us up to Astley Bridge Park and our special place. We cried over everything we expected would happen, but hoped and prayed wouldn't. We talked about good times, too. I questioned her again about where she had been, but even then, when she would be leaving forever, she still couldn't say. She leaned forward and kissed me on the lips. She'd kissed me before, but nothing like that last one. It was different from anything before. While we hugged, something just took over me, and I realised that she was the one person I could trust not to hurt me. Without thinking, I kissed her neck. It was all over inside an hour. That was it: my very best friend, gone, and it was back to being just me and my wall.

24

ONE STEP FORWARD, TWO STEPS BACK

Summer Holiday 1963

My new friend, Kevin, was earning two shillings sixpence a day helping deliver fresh bread from the big bakery to the local bread shops. "Anyone can do it," he said, when I asked how he got the job. "You just wait near the big doors and the driver will pick you."

Standing at the big double doors, the warm sweet smell of fresh loaves wiped my nose again and again. I couldn't get enough of the way it filled my nostrils and pulled all the juices down from the roof of my mouth ready to taste... until diesel fumes stunk it away. A dozen other kids were also waiting for a bread van to choose them. The boy nearest the folding doors held up his arm long enough for a driver to accept him.

"Never climb into a car with someone you don't know," Mum's words I ignored when a fourth driver stopped long enough for me to climb in. The cabin of the van smelled of bread with a touch of aftershave.

Kitty's Diary

August 1963

Peter keeps talking about the bread vans. Don't know who they are, could be anyone. I've told him no.

The driver with the belly: smartly dressed, shaven, and hair greased with a parting axed down the left side. He was smart—*really* smart—as if he was going out dancing. We introduced ourselves and he asked which team I supported. I told him Bolton Wanderers, and boasted I was going to be goalkeeper, like Eddie. He didn't respond. Instead, there was silence as the tarmac road notched us up to fifty miles an hour. For reasons I don't understand to this day, I suddenly said, "I like watching Steve Reeves in 'Hercules Unchained'. I even went on to inform him that Hercules was the son of Zeus—thunderbolt-throwing king of the sky. And about Zeus's other son, Hermes—god of travel and travellers, and also bit of a con artist.

"You must always have your nose in a book."

"Steve Reeves taught me."

"Who?"

"Film star, Steve Reeves."

There was a long silence, before he called out, "First stop. Get fifteen of the red—medium slice. Then ten of the blue—thick slice, from the top shelf."

"Come on, *ten* of the wraps!" he said impatiently.

I had picked out five of the blues when a hole in my head opened up, pushing all my numbers out: six, seven, eight, and nine all plopped onto the pavement. Ten stayed on the edge of my brain. *Never mind,* I thought. *Right, shift the twenty-five reds and twenty blues to the bottom tray for the next drop.* It looked so right. I was feeling great—I was going to be earning pocket money like all the other kids. But he came back asking why I had put the wrong bread in the wrong places. I wasn't understanding anything that he was asking of me. In that moment, it was as if every part of the van, including all the bread, had just disappeared. Gone. I wanted my head back. I wanted the hole that was draining everything out glued and sealed back up. I just wanted a head like all the other heads, instead of me just standing there on the pavement, wondering how the other kids did it and why I couldn't. I wanted my inner chest and stomach to change, too, to relax. To get rid of the sickly feeling and funny colours. I wanted to keep my head lit up, instead of being taken over with a sudden blackness that refused to let me think. I wanted the light switching back on, so I could see all of my thoughts as I used to. Somehow, my head just didn't look like theirs.

At home that night, sleep tried its best, but lost, taken over by bright electric sparks birthing up all the day's problems. I didn't understand why numbers and logic had just left me. The next morning, tired, I was back at the bakery gates for six a.m. I waited there until all the other boys arrived, but I was left behind. It would be the same on every drop for the next week. I was there, six o'clock, every morning, waiting with all the other boys, and every morning I was rejected.

"You won't be coming again," shouted the driver. It was back home for me. I spent a couple of hours in the coal shed trying to make words with John Bull, wearing a kid's gas mask. It smelled of the dentist, so I snapped it off and lobbed it to the back of the coal shed where it rested, bored, until my next happening. As always, there was silence. I often wondered why there was never such a loud silence in other people's houses, on those rare occasions I ever went into any of them.

The stone-flagged floors were walking Dad's hobnailed boots toward me. "What's wrong?" I raised my brows and shrugged my shoulders. I wanted to ask why I wasn't like the other boys—how I could do things most other kids couldn't, yet I couldn't do some of the simple things all the other kids could. My mind felt ready, but my tongue wouldn't carry the words. I could feel them stack up round the back of my throat ready to set on fire. Heartburn. Indigestion. All of those uncomfortable things held together, as tight as tight, in my sheer frustration. I just couldn't find the strength or confidence to speak.

He clutched my bag of marbles, which were on the table wearing coal dust, then bent down and started thumbing and flicking each of them. I knew what he wanted me to do: one, two, three, four… up to fifteen. Out of the blue, he said, "Forget what happened with the bread van. He's an idiot. No one likes him." I asked how he knew it had all gone wrong, but he just changed the subject. His marble was the first in the chalked circle. I realised, then, more than any other time, that Dad and I were friends. I felt safe with him. I think he knew deep down there was something different about me and the way I was. Somehow, he seemed to understand. Regardless of his Victorian hang-ups, we were friends. Good friends. It wasn't his fault he had been born in 1895, with all those horrific attitudes forced upon him and his peers, being brainwashed into believing that all the faults of the world were caused by alcohol. That's just how it was.

Ours was a game to end all games. Dad must have been a marble champion in his childhood, beating me the way he did. I knew little about him: there were no old photos, no talk of his childhood, school, or first jobs. Only that he had a son called Stanley who had been a scale fitter and rode a BSA dual exhaust motorcycle. That was all he ever told me.

Kitty's Diary

He can't stop talking about O'Hara winning—breaking that other boy's nose. He won't go down that fighting road. I won't let him.

It was on a rare morning that Dad was off work, the time he walked me down to Len Tobutts' sports shop. The windows and walls inside were completely covered with gear for every type of sport played at that time, and many that weren't.

Dad and the owner were chatting for a few minutes before I was shown some big, leather-toed boots, just like the ones Stanley Matthews wore. Yes, they were good!

"No," Dad said. "There's a pair of continental boots in the window, the ones with sloping toes and rubber studs."

Silence.

"No need to fold your arms like that," he continued. "We've known each other for too long."

Silence.

"Never mind the cost," the owner told him, "we can sort it later."

Kitty's Diary
October 1963

How has he managed to get Peter a paper round when everyone's said, 'No paper boys needed'? Peter really loves his baking.

Paper Round

The price of everything was going up. I needed to do that paper round. Mr. Joseph, the newsagent owner, brought in one of the boys to show me the directions. Everything was fine until I was left on my own. For some reason, as soon as I stepped onto Windermere Street, my left and right disappeared. Gone. My very own left and right had deserted me. I was in the middle of nowhere. Alone, I was lost in the middle of everywhere. I'd walked those streets hundreds of times. I knew all the street names. If anyone asked me for directions, I could always point them in the right direction. Not anymore. I returned to the paper shop with the undelivered papers.

Later, Mr. Joseph had to send someone round to see if I was okay. I was soon back on the round with Tony, the same boy who had rescued me when I hadn't understood the door numbering or street names. Together, we delivered the rest of the papers.

"I thought you'd got lost," said Mr. Joseph. "People have been in asking about their papers…"

Kitty's Diary

Twice now, he's finished early to walk with Peter on his paper round.

Bike

My savings were growing, and I had my eye on the bike in Kay's on Halliwell Road. The bike with finger-thin tyres, yellow and black frame, derailleur gears, hanging above the counter on the back wall. Two months later it was mine, even though I hadn't paid for it all; Dad paid off the last five pounds.

It was the bike of all bikes. The word 'excitement' doesn't even come close. It was like that for weeks until, for reasons only Dad knew, he started saying girls would be more interested in me now, because of my bike. Of course, it was a joke. "You'll pay for the rest of your life if you get a girl into trouble." I didn't know about this 'trouble'.

"You shouldn't be saying things like that to him!" Mum would call out.

Dad suggested we spend the afternoon out, just me and him. From Bolton Station we caught the number 15 bus to Wigan. Our first stop was Aspull, where I was born. We walked up High Lane and then down Copperas Lane, where Mum used to pram me with other single mothers when there were no other families near us. We stopped at the ghost house of Haigh Hall with its six open-wide pillars. I charged over to the miniature railway as Dad paid the entrance and stood waiting with his Woodbines, teeth in, blue trilby partly covering his white hair. One hand was hidden inside his long coat. I'd never seen him that relaxed before. Later on, we skimmed pebbles along the Leeds and Liverpool Canal, near Water Street. It was our only day out together. All the way home, we talked bikes.

Christmas 1963

Kitty's Diary

December 1963

He's going blind. Doctor said the fires are to blame. Won't spoil Peter's Christmas—I shall tell him in the new year that we have to move house.

That Christmas seemed to be the beginning, or end, of something. It was strange: there were more presents than ever before. The pair of cycle toeclips, along with shoes to fit. The stack of presents: a football, cycling and swimming gear, and a really heavy present wrapped in lots of birthday paper. I'd never had such a heavy gift. There it was—an eighteen inch square of marble. "All the best bakers use marble to roll out their pastry on!" Within minutes, we were all crying happy tears. Life was good at 339 Blackburn Road; it was the place to be.

Kitty's Diary

January 1964

Told Peter his dad's going blind. He cried all night.

I became so stressed just at the thought of metalwork and woodwork class. It had become my most hated class, while all others loved it more than anything. "So, you want to be a baker and confectioner?" asked Mr. Burns, the headmaster, who finally gave me permission to take cooking classes instead.

It was a one-to-one session with the teacher in her spare time. Some things you never forget. There was an instant liking to her, not just for working with me, but because I felt she accepted me. There was an instant feeling of home. I slipped on my homemade white apron that Mum had helped me to make, and I was ready to go. Our first bake was a large bread loaf. Again, that smell of warm bread and the way it fills your nose. Then there's the anticipation. The first taste, like nothing I had tasted before, and *I* had made it. The first of many. Mum wanted to buy me a wicker basket, similar to the ones the girls used to bring their baking home in. No. Instead it was a brown paper bag to keep the goodies warm. Yes, we preferred the brown bag.

Kitty's Diary

Being retired should be the best time. All that coal dust, down in that fire-hole where very few ever went down, and Thomas can't cope without it.

25

LEAVING BLACKBURN ROAD

My bike and I put together a programme to keep us really fit, with football and cycling wherever and whenever we could find time. There was nothing stopping us, no excuses: it was up to us. We trained while we waited to be scouted for a league. Any league team would do, for the start. Wherever that was going to be, my bike would be with me. It's how we were: inseparable. We were made for each other. Of course, Dad ummed and ahhed about my programme, asking 'would it be too much' for me. But, finally, he agreed.

Biking it to school, everyone wanted to know about my bike, with its drop handlebars, derailleur gears, and finger-thin racing wheels. The girls wanted to try it out. I was sharing my bike with Susan Crook and Katherine Duckworth. They were the best-looking of all the girls; even the other girls seemed jealous of them. Wednesday at school was cooking day, and I would ride home one-handed whilst carrying my cakes made from class in the other.

Life was good.

Kitty's Diary
April 1964

Landlord wants us out. Thomas has been here since the war! Our home. He offered us the chance to buy it for £250. Thomas declined, saying no way—we are Labour and working class.

Dad's eyes were now getting so bad he was sitting just four feet from the telly, leaning back so as not to get in the way of anyone. With Dad no longer working, little money was coming in, but we weren't stressed about it. Dad said it was a short-term thing, since I would soon be signing for a professional team—maybe Bolton! Meanwhile, I was playing for both the Lads Club A team and also The Bolton Catholic Boys, all organised by our school sports teacher, Mr. Lomax. People were noticing how much my goalkeeping was improving, especially when I made it into the Bolton Saturday Sport, 'The Buff', again.

"I can't live off wishes and recommendations," said our landlord. I'll never forget his nose: long, and thin enough to pick a lock. He gave us a month to vacate the house. Dad had been there nearly thirty years, since the landlord's father had owned it. They couldn't do this to him—*could* they? They did.

People I had never heard of or seen before came to the house to collect whatever. Groups, pawn shop owners. We had a big fire in the back garden on the opposite side to where Vick was buried. I didn't want to leave him. I wanted to dig him up and put him on the fire. "No, don't do that!" Dad said. "Just remember him how he was." I cried. I hadn't a clue where we were going, only that it was a two-bedroom flat. The amount of stuff that had been collected over the years was incredible. Dad gave loads to a Jamaican family he knew from the mill who hadn't been over long. The mother was pushing her baby, who was sucking on a large mango stone because they were teething. I laughed, thinking it so strange, because I'd never seen anything like it before.

I spent those last few days going through the half-empty house, saying goodbye to all the rooms and tapping all the walls. I was convinced there was a room I hadn't found yet. Another secret room. I searched and searched, but nothing. I even searched the outside toilet, rubbing my hands all over the whitewashed walls. Nothing. I was going to leave that house without ever finding my *own* secret room. I went outside and said my goodbyes to Vick.

I wondered how Rachel would find me. When I asked Mum, I didn't expect, "If she's a real friend, she'll find you. You're forgetting she's getting on for twenty! You need to stop bothering about her. She's probably engaged or even married to someone by now." I wrote my new address, **116 Wilkinson Gardens, Oldhams Estate**, in large red letters on a white piece of paper and handed it to Mrs. Murray. She owned the off-licence next door to us. She knew both Rachel and her mum.

116 Wilkinson Gardens was a block of flats and we were sat at the top. Dad was okay about it; so, too, were me and Mum. It was my bike who didn't like it. It suddenly became very heavy and stubborn, dragging its wheels over every one of those thirty stone steps. Yes, it was probably tired—old, even. We were coming to realise we had outgrown each other. We had shared good times, but its eighteen-inch frame was getting too small for me. I had been saving whatever I could.

It was the weekend after the holidays and there, in our front room, stood a Falcon Black Diamond bike. Mum and Dad hadn't said anything. Where and how they came to get it was beyond me. It must have cost them thirty, maybe forty, pounds. That Falcon Black Diamond was the most beautiful thing I had ever seen. I had something like five pounds saved, which I tried to give to Dad. He wouldn't accept it. He found a good home for my old bike—a boy down by Lee Clough Mission in Old Road; Taylor, I think his name was.

I had started lifting weights and my arms were getting stronger. I kept telling Mum I was all right and that I wouldn't hurt myself 'down there'.

Kitty's Diary

April 1964

Peter will be all right. He'll still see all his friends.
Oldhams estate is only a two-minute bike ride away.

Paul Smith, a chubby lad with Brylcreemed hair, knocked on the door for me—goalkeeper in their knockabout team. He was one of maybe half a dozen who came on a regular basis, looking for my goalie skills, and now I was deserting them with no time to explain. Dad kept saying that if they thought a lot of me, they'd find me. I wanted to stay at 339 Blackburn Road like I never wanted anything before. But there was no time to think of friends from the Blackburn Road area.

I wanted that large Victorian house I grew up in. I wanted all its secrets, good and bad. I wanted like I had never wanted anything before. I wanted the coal shed where I had spent much of my childhood. The most traumatic of all was leaving my wall and my outside toilet, where I had learnt and practised all by myself to become football and marble champion of Blackburn Road. All those years afraid of the cellar and the shadow of a man I saw as I stood watching over Dad's shoulder, kept awake most nights and wanting to ask who he was, but fearing the answer.

"You need to go down into the cellar to sort things out," said Mum. "See what can be taken down to Maxi's. Tell him we don't want anything for it, not after all he's done for us over the years."

"What things?" I didn't know what was down there. I tried my hardest not to go down!

"Please, Peter!" Mum insisted.

Before I could object, I noticed Dad was crying. "Okay, I'll go down. I'll sort everything." I took his bunch of keys and, like Dad, whistled off the dust. Loud creaking opened the door to a wall of black as I pushed the cold breathing to one side. Going down into the cellar was scary; it was everything I thought it would be. Okay, the yellow circle from the ceiling light cut out a large chunk of black, but it was quickly fading, with still a way to go before stepping into more black. Fright made me stop still. Where was Rachel? I needed her more than ever before. I sucked in a piece of the yellow through my teeth. Bottom of the stairs, more black, until the light switch finally caught my finger.

The stench of damp in the cellar wiped my nose. I shuddered, wiping away the cobwebs from my face and shoulders. The yellow light was bouncing down, down, stopping just short of the far wall. I saw no man there. Breathing easier, my feet and I moved forward. Suddenly, in the far corner, just inside the black, a figure! My head and I didn't want this, but my body, well! My *body* was a different kettle of fish. My body loved testing itself—a *real* adventurer. I stood firm and blasted the figure with the full beam of Dad's extra-powerful policeman torch. Standing before me was a creepy mannequin dressed in First World War uniform. A gush of cold monster breath hit me out of nowhere and my tingling legs were urging me to *run*, but my head decided to tough it out.

The mannequin was the stranger who I had seen all those years ago. There it was, a six foot being who had given me years of nightmares filled with monsters and gangsters, as well as drowning and falling from cliffs. Now, there he was, just stepping out of the black like that, and, oddly, it made me feel safe. All those years of childhood fear wasted on one stupid mannequin.

My anger stayed silent.

A dust-covered workbench to my left held up every building tool you would ever need. Next to it, with their feet up in the air, were a dozen or so iron shoe lasts of all shapes and sizes. Draining rods were hanging overhead, between the cobwebs. To my right was a clean portmanteau, its locks clicked and the pushed-up lid pulling out bunches of black and white photos. The picture of a man and boy standing next to each other, and, beside them, a fully-grown Alsatian. There was a young boy's clothes in a pile on the cellar floor. Another picture of the boy, hair like mine—black as a blackboard. He was wearing a gas mask and playing with a John Bull printing set. Dad's handwriting on the back, 'Happy birthday, Stanley! Now you're in double figures'. And another: '21st! Happy birthday. 22nd December 1948'. Three days before mine. All the photos of the boy were just like me; we could have been twins. Also waiting on the sides of the case were a pair of kiddie's shoes, eager to step out. Underneath the shoes were an assortment of boys' clothes, with shoes to match, all getting ready to play. Footy, cricket, whatever, they were eager for their time out of that case. In the corner was a picture of an old tricycle with a hinged box on the back. Just like mine, save for my Saint Christopher bell. Whose trike was it? Everything there was a version of me, but not me. The cellar was shouting about being lonely.

26

EPILEPSY

Dad seemed upset, the way he did when he was about to cry. In his lap was the gift from the cotton mill, where he had worked for so long: a box of one hundred Woodbines and a cigarette lighter. Mum glared at it in disgust and began shouting about his forty-three years and *just* a box of cigarettes. Dad finally started crying; I guessed more out of anger than anything else. I ran back upstairs to the yellow door and stepped into a room with just a single bed and a wooden stool holding up an alarm clock set for five-thirty a.m. The walls were white with one picture of a young man standing in front of a motorbike and sidecar. I couldn't help but stare at it. The sidecar I was taken for a ride in when I about four years old. It was a ride up to a not-long-built housing estate called Oldhams. There were net curtains hiding a clear look of the back yard. There was no rug on the bare wooden floorboards. There was nothing in there.

Mum shouted me downstairs. I saw Dad giving all his tools to Dennis Smith, a young plumber who lived a few yards from us. Dad was still crying. There was a strange nakedness to the house. The 'removal van' was a coal wagon that had been washed down before coming to our house. They were men I had seen before. I went to the wall and the outside toilet to thank them for being there whenever I had needed them.

"Bert," said Dad, "Take us to 116 Wilkinson Gardens, Oldhams Estate." He didn't even look back. I watched 339 Blackburn Road slide into the distance.

Kitty's Diary

Peter won't say why he spends so much time on the veranda. Why would he want to keep counting the number of houses in each of the rows?

A new beginning. Our flat, 116, was on the top flight with no lift. It was fine for me. The veranda was brilliant. I was missing my wall, but I was excited about starting work and the chance at being signed up to a club.

That July, our bus driver on the way home had to stop three times to sort out my excitement. We were almost home when a strange smell of wood started burning my nose, but there were no fires about. Then, there was a 'click' deep down inside my head and a tingle ran up from out of the ground, through my shoe, then up my right leg. I took a mint from my pocket, put the paper in my mouth, then threw away the mint. My mouth was drier than dry.

Bolton Infirmary woke me up, my tongue burning with pain. "Epilepsy," said the doctor. "Peter's not to get too excited." Mum had to console Dad, he was so upset.

Kitty's Diary
August 1964

Epilepsy killed his little brother Henry, before the war. Only nine, he was.

Mum had to tell Dad to stop fussing, as it would make things worse, and could make me ill again. I had stopped being me and the new me was aching. All I could remember was the other kids on the bus talking about the last days of school and wondering what was to come next.

The hospital gave me anti-epileptic drugs.

Six weeks later, there was a knock on the door asking if I could be goalkeeper in the Sunday League in two weeks' time. A game on Barlow Park, just a ten-minute walk from our house. I said yes without thinking. Dad wasn't sure. Mum was totally against it.

Everything was back to normal. The dark goalkeeper

jumper was back on; so too were the slim boots which helped win the Bolton Wanderers Cup. The pitch was good. Everything was how it should be. The referee was in his black gear, as were his linesmen. We even had nets, hanging on for dear life from the crossbar. Everything was good. Balls were coming from every direction and I was having the best time; there was clapping for my saves and a few pats on the back.

1-0 to us.

Half time: orange segments. We were doing good. The game was ours.

Second half. A slow easy ball came in. I dived after it. In the net.

1-1.

Something seemed to be holding me back. I was becoming slower.

2-1 to them.

A corner kick to them. I knew what I had to do: leap up and punch it away.

3-1

Then came a strong smell of bread. My leg was tingling; my brain was fizzing.

I woke in my bed. Mum was in the bedroom, and so was the guy who had knocked on our door asking me to play for their team: he had brought me home in his car after the match. Mum and Dad were whispering. I started crying, more than any other time. I knew bad news was coming.

"You can't use your bike again," muttered Dad, "it's too dangerous." The man left, wishing me good luck. Then Dad started crying too. Mum sat down on the bed and told me that football was not good for me, either, and that I would have to give it up. I never heard from the man again. I knew there would never be another knock on the door, and I was right.

27

TRAFFIC JAM

Kitty's Diary

September 1964

Peter's very nervous. He'll be all right at the bakery—
they'll look after him. He wouldn't have me making sure he
got there on time, but I went down, anyway.

Dad and the tall ginger-haired manager, Mr. Benson, nodded
to each other. I thought nothing of it. Why would I? The
hot smell of freshly made bakes smelt my nose. There were
three long, wide steel tables with bakers either side working
pies, cakes, and bread.

"You're looking nervous," said Mr. Wilkinson, a large-
bellied guy in charge of delivery. We shook hands. "You'll
be okay."

We were at the back of the delivery van. "See," he said. "If the trays are at the back, just get this long hook and pull them out. Easy."

There was silence while I gathered my thoughts.

By the afternoon, I was at the tables making dough for the pies. With that done, I had to clean out the returned metal pie dishes. Apart from the older man, there was Danny, who was on the ovens. I was the only male working in the bigger confectionery section of the bakery. The rest were all middle-aged women, the sort of hard women you don't mess with. The women who had been working in the cotton mills until redundancy. There was one—just one—young woman called Jane, maybe eighteen, working on the jam section, who just took my breath away. I couldn't stop looking at her. Every time I had to get something from the other side of the bakery, I would pass her by, brushing back my hair as she brushed jam across a long line of puff pastry. I would get as close as I could, and each time, she would smile.

Silence.

I wanted to ask her out, but my mouth wouldn't work.

Kitty's Diary

Those mill girls teasing Peter again. Sending him to ask that pretty Jane to fill an empty tin with 'traffic jam'! Will have to have words.

I was so embarrassed with everyone laughing at me for a tin full of 'traffic jam'. Dad had only warned me about going for a 'bucket of steam' or a 'glass hammer'. But, of course, none of that counted in a bakery. I somehow didn't want to be with them. It just didn't feel right. My escape was the delivery van, going out to all our shops around Bolton. Every morning, I was off with Jack, delivering pies and cakes to each of the six shops around town; he showed me everything and introduced me to all the staff.

Kitty's Diary

He doesn't understand pranks. They were doing what they've always done with young boys. Just one of those things.

Three days later, the prank was still hitting my embarrassment when Pat, one of the mill girls, came over, "We're all going to the baths after work tomorrow." She smiled at me with a wink, "Jane's coming…" All the other women were looking over and nodding their heads.

Thursday afternoon. Work finished. The women were all leaving their workbenches to go into the coatroom when Jane walked over. "Are you coming swimming?" she said, headed for the door.

Then Pat came over, too. "Where's your swimming stuff?"
Silence.

***

The next day, I was preparing pie pastry. Mr. Benson lifted a huge chunk of dough from the mixing machine and flopped it onto the steel table. "Easy. Just cut and weigh out two pounds." He did a couple, each side of the two pound mark. Scales and I couldn't get it together. We tried; we gave it our best. That afternoon, the other workers' eyes covered me, head to foot. I moved everything down the end of the table, as far as I could go. They seemed to move closer. My mouth was dry as could be. I kept visiting the toilet. Colours were hitting my eyes, and a silver tingling was running up my leg.

Next thing I knew, I was in the hospital again, Mr. Benson at my bedside. Silence. I'd bitten my tongue. My legs were hurting. "You should have told us you had epilepsy."

***

Back in the bakery, everyone was asking me how I felt and what it was like having epilepsy. "My uncle's second cousin had it; killed him in his sleep."

Silence blew out the windows.

I'd been in the bakery six weeks, but dough and I were still not getting it together, so Sheila was sent down to help. She was one of those mill women who had teased and teased, but she just smiled, asked if I was okay, and then carried on with the dough making. Her sideways glance came every five minutes. The teasing had stopped. Strange—I missed it. It wasn't going to happen.

Escape, as usual, was with Jack on the delivery van. He became my confidant. He would stop the van halfway round our delivery route. I don't even remember him ever saying, 'Right, I'm listening'. No, he never asked, but, somehow, he knew. Sometimes, he would have to wait there half an hour before I started telling him how difficult I was finding it at the bakery. I tried explaining the problems of weighing of the dough. How I wasn't used to scales, and the confusion with numbers and cutting the dough into equal sizes. I didn't understand what 'equal sizes' was. How, even when it seemed so right to me, it always turned out to be wrong. He never laughed, and never judged. He was always just Jack being Jack. A guy who I think had seen and heard everything any human being possibly could. We would then carry on delivering as though nothing had happened—he was like that.

Kitty's Diary

October 1964

Told Peter to take no notice of his Dad's nonsense about women taking advantage of young boys.

Mum was giving me two shillings and sixpence a day for dinner money, but, delivering pies and cakes to the various shops, I soon learnt that, if any of the pies were damaged in transit, they would get thrown away. So, instead of spending the dinner money, I started hitting a few pies with the rod used for pulling out trays. I'd eat those pies for my dinner and save the shillings for a rainy day. I became a dead shot, hitting which ever pie or cake I fancied, just enough that the shops would refuse them. A pie a day, alongside a chocolate eclair.

Me, the meat pies, and those chocolate cream cakes loved each other. I never disappointed myself or the cakes—we just got it together. Jack, a sergeant major from the war, would only shout my wrongs whilst in the van. I saved up that dinner money to pay for my nightly visits to Hollywood: *Magnificent Seven*, *Frankenstein*, *Three Stooges*, *Meet the Mum*…

I was cleaning out pie tins when the tingling came back. Colours I'd never seen before were hitting both my eyes and filling my head. The tingling was moving up my leg.

Up, up, and up.

I woke in hospital with Jack sat next to my bed, his eyes red and watery. A bruise from the steel table pained my head.

***

A few days later. "I'm sorry, Peter," said Mr. Benson, "we can't keep you on; it's too dangerous with all this machinery."

Mum helped collect all the tears I dropped that day.

"It's okay," Dad said. "It's not your fault."

Alone, I walked around our estate. Alone, but not lonely. Coffee smelt my nose, yet there was nobody drinking it.

28

THE BUTCHERY

An appointment at the Labour Exchange arrived in a brown envelope, warning me not to be late. But it's impossible for me to be late. Being late, or anyone else being late, especially when a time has been arranged, completely freaks me out. It almost sends me into meltdown. Waiting also sends me into that dark place, but not as fast.

Fifteen minutes, I sat there, waiting for the careers officer in a small green room where posters of young farmers, calves around their shoulders, were walking towards me. A red pain was now inching into my brain, anger sweating my hands as I rubbed my knees. Finally, the tall officer, with the mustard tie vomiting down his shirt and Brylcreemed hair and axe parting to one side, pulled up his chair to within a few inches of mine. I didn't understand the brutal expression on his face.

Silence while he thumbed through a folder.

"On your chosen jobs you've ticked: footballer, forester, and postman."

"Why are you smiling like that?" I asked him.

"Your worksheet says you were sacked." There was a long pause before he continued. "So, you've been diagnosed with epilepsy; you can barely read and write; you can't do any maths; and you want to be a postman or a forester? Never. They only employ those who can read and know their maths. You can't do any of those things."

Silence.

"Stop rubbing your legs like that. It's distracting and it won't get you anywhere." I settled down and stopped rubbing my leg, but then he put his hand on it. Shocked, it took me a few seconds to realise what was happening and to move my leg away. I slid my chair back as he turned to pull a card from his desk drawer.

"There's a job for a young labourer in a butcher's, carrying meat from store to wagon. You can have that." I stared at the man who apparently didn't seem to think my epilepsy would be an issue. "Why are you looking like that? It's a job, isn't it? You do know where Thine Street is, don't you? It's after the train station. You can just ask someone if you get lost."

Butchery Week One

There were no introductions. The giant man on the upper level of the bone yard just shouted, "Get yourself a white coat, then straight back."

The white coat was two sizes too big. "They call me Big Les," the man said, hauling a long hind side of beef. Then he lifted and carried a full-sized pig under his arm. "Get the other pig! So, what do they call you?"

"Peter."

"You're the kid who has fits?"

Silence.

I followed him into the main section where Billy, the foreman, showed me how to slice and pull apart the white membrane of a large piece of silverside beef. My turn. I just had to slice down while opening up the silver streak, shaving through the beef. Easy. He gave me the next one, but the phone was asking for him. "Get on with it." A couple of minutes later, the phone was after him again: he tried escaping, but it eventually got him, and he left me with five more cuts to do.

Big Les looked down at me from up on the landing, as I wandered around, looking lost. "Finished already?" The others gathered round my table to watch me. Some nodded, while others just went back to their own table. "Good," the boss shouted down, "now start on the next one." Ten minutes later, the phone let go of him. He shouted and cursed, finally pushing me to one side, screaming about it being a *very* expensive piece of beef. The other workers started to laugh and cheer. One of them lay down on the floor, mimicking my epileptic seizure. I forced myself not to cry.

"Leave the boy alone," shouted Henry, a sturdy black guy working on the bench right at the back.

"It's just a bit of fun, that's all."

"He's only a kid," he said, before two of the other workers set about beating him to the floor. A third, Terry, charged in and kicked Henry in the head. Then they all went back to their benches.

As I went over to help him up off the floor, Terry stepped between us. "It's nothing to do with you," he shouted, loud enough so that everyone could hear. "If he had just stayed in Jamaica," he added, before they all started singing 'Jolly Good Company'.

***

A couple of weeks later, I met with an old school friend, Cornelius. Someone who always seemed different from the rest, including me. Over the next few months, he would introduce me to the 'Gaff lads'—fairground workers and other men who had been, or were still, bareknuckle fighters, ex-soldiers, and travellers. Those friends of his were strange, hard, always in clothes which had seen better days. Yet they always had huge wads of ten pound notes, enough to choke a donkey. It was Cornelius who helped me out with the odd day's work on the fairground.

I was on the ping-pong stall, charging punters threepence a go. '**Win a teddy bear or dolly of your choice. Thruppence a go—land the ping-pong ball on the plate and make it stay. Come on, just thruppence a go!**' I would turn, spit on the ball and stick it on the plate, otherwise it was impossible for it to stay put.

A couple of times, when I went into seizure, those hard guys on the edges of society would stay with me, not letting anyone make fun or abuse me in any way. They once even took me home. Mum wasn't sure about them, especially when one asked, "Where's your toilet? I need to empty my clog." Dad just smirked and made them a cup of tea. They shared Woodbines. Once tea was drunk, they left.

I didn't know what to expect when I told Cornelius and the lads about the bullying at work. At first there was talk of breaking Terry's legs. No. Of course, I thought he was joking, but it frightened me, almost as much as going to work every day and having to face Terry and the rest. I was also frightened for Henry and the beating he would get if he came to my rescue again. There would be even more broken legs.

Mick O'Hara gave me his knuckleduster. I was to keep it

in my pocket at all times, just in case. Three weeks, it stayed calm, redundant in my front apron pocket. It was safe there. I hadn't to lose it—'insurance', as O'Hara put it. But I had to get out: it wasn't me, the beatings, threats, bullying. I took an extra hour off at lunch to visit the employment office, where, once again, they would be asking what I had done wrong. Me. It was always *me*. Never anyone else. I started to tell them everything about the place. He shut me up before I had the chance to tell him about the beatings. He didn't believe me and just told me to stop complaining.

Kitty's Diary

November 1964

Peter's not saying anything. There's something wrong. He's not talking. Stays in his room.

That evening, Dad asked if everything was okay. Each time, I gave the same nod, followed by, "It's good."

"You don't look 'okay'," Mum would say. Dinner on the table. Her arms folded, waiting to hear my happenings, both good and bad, of the day. Of course she knew there was something wrong. She was my Mum. I was careful to miss out Terry cutting up a piece of fat, used for making glue, and shoving it in my mouth. Henry had come to my rescue. Again, he was set upon.

Silence.

***

Back in work, after the foreman sent me to the other side of the bone yard to help load all the bins, Terry asked for my help in the freezers on the second floor. The freezer was almost the size of a penalty area, with giant icicles holding up the roof. He was carrying another full pig under his arm. Inside the freezer, he ordered me to take the pig over to the far side and stack it on top of the pile already there. Suddenly, he knocked the ceiling hard with a huge brush-headed broom, covering me with ice, and laughed at me trying to brush it off.

"Hurry up," he shouted, headed for the big door. I was about a yard from him when he gave out a weird laugh, switched off the light and slammed the door shut, leaving me inside the freezer. I wasn't going to shout and plead. I was going to stay there and be silent. I wasn't going to show fright, even though I was terrified. I didn't know if it was the fright or the cold making me shiver. I ran my hand over the area where I thought the light switch was. It was so dark. I just couldn't find it. Knowing them, they'd be behind the door, waiting for me to cry or scream, or both. It wasn't going to happen. I wasn't to panic; someone would come and find me. Terry wouldn't let me die, would he? He wouldn't forget.

I was tired and my fingers were so cold they were burning.

Frost had now soaked through my clothes. I jumped up and down, rubbed my legs and arms, blew on my hands. The freeze was grabbing hold. I was finding it hard to move, but I knew I had to keep moving the best I could, hoping there was nothing around me I might trip over. The grip of the freeze was tightening, when the door finally opened and a yellow light cut out a big chunk of the dark. A broad-shouldered black guy stood there shaking his head. "Don't let them get to you," he said in his strong Caribbean accent. I still wasn't going to cry.

"Are you bloody stupid?" the foreman screamed at me. "You could have died. If you carry on like this, you will be finished." I was going to shout out that it was Terry, when he just pushed past Henry and said, "Why didn't you hit the bell?"

"I couldn't find it in the dark."

"You switched it off *before* you closed the door?"

Silence.

"Only babies cry," he said, tutting as he walked off.

Downstairs, Terry was drinking a mug of tea. "You look *cold*."

"That's it," said the foreman. "The kid's had enough." I had to stop myself from crying again.

"Come on," Henry said, "get yourself a hot drink, and you'll be okay." Hot cups of tea were trying their best to warm me when Marie, a slim girl with hair in a bob, was trying not to attract attention as she walked past us.

"Are you going to sort this one out?" Terry shouted. The other guys were laughing.

"Piss off," she shouted back.

He forced a smile, "She's had more pricks than a second-hand dartboard." Her flying cup just missed him. He laughed. More swearing and laughter was aimed at me again, making fun of me being in the freezer. I didn't even feel my fingers slipping into the leaded knuckleduster which the Gaffs had moulded around my clenched fist. He was laughing when I swung out and hit him in the face. I'd never seen a broken jaw before. I'd never heard a grown man scream like a baby before. I ran like I had never run before.

Friends found me in the Griffin. I talked them through what had happened. I explained that the butchers knew where I lived. They heard my fright about going to the police. Slim, tall Pete Munro laughed, "Police. No. There'll be no police." He smiled a strange smile. The others nodded. Nothing more was said, and I wasn't going to ask, so left it at that.

That same day, a note was passed to me saying I had been sacked from the butcher's, because it was 'too dangerous for someone with epilepsy'.

29

SANDRA

My whole life had died within a matter of weeks. Gone were my dreams of goalkeeping. I was fifteen with nowhere to go; everything about me was dying. I wanted to escape on my bike, but Mum had chained it to the radiator until she could find a good home for it.

I was sent to the Co-op as a milk boy, but got sacked for crashing into a brick wall while driving the milk cart.

Alliance Cash and Carry—sacked after my epilepsy let me down in the aisle while dealing with customers.

Yates delivery service—sacked after a seizure while carrying a crate of wine.

Mum kept asking what was wrong. My life, in two years, had changed beyond belief. Dad suggested I take my ball for a kickabout on my own in Barlow Park. Give the ball a breather after being under the bed for so many weeks. It was then that I met a tall, blonde guy called Roy, who also seemed always to be on his own. We became friends. There was no pressure of meeting up at set times: if he turned up, fine; if he didn't, also fine.

1st March 1967

One day, a few years later, Roy suggested going down to the Palais. He talked about a girl he had just met and that he'd arranged to meet her there, right of the bandstand, at eight. I had always thought you would meet a girl outside and both go in together.

He pointed to the staggeringly beautiful brunette waiting by the stage, wearing a light green pleated skirt and dark green top. He said he was lucky to get a kiss, never mind anything else. He shrugged his shoulders like it, or she— whoever she was—didn't really matter. I waited next to her while he went to get a drink for the both of them. Nobody spoke until he returned to announce that a fight was expected later with some rival footballers, and he asked if I could walk his girlfriend to the bus stop. I thought he was joking.

No. He hurried away. She was on the verge of crying when I introduced myself and asked her name.

"Sandra." I waited for her to follow with a few more words. There weren't any. I walked her to the bus stop and made sure she got on the bus.

The following week, he asked me again to take her to the bus stop. Sandra and I stood next to each other, wondering what to say. The week after that, it happened again, and I finally just took hold of her and kissed her. She kissed me back.

We had been dating a few weeks when my epilepsy kicked in. At the hospital, I woke to find her crying. We survived that first seizure. But two days following another episode, when we were supposed to be meeting in Bolton, I had waited and waited, when eventually she came running, crying, saying her mother had hidden the key to her wardrobe. After a long silence, she had told her mother she would run away if she wasn't given her key.

September 1967

Sandra accepted my marriage proposal. We both agreed I wouldn't be able to get a mortgage on my seven pounds per week at the Co-op. The following month, Mrs. Jones, disability officer at the Job Centre, found me work as a gravedigger. I was to start two weeks later.

30

MUM

4th April 1998

On the lawn under the front room window, there was an assortment of wreaths and flowers. She wouldn't have liked them. 'Waste of money!' she would have said. She'd have gone with plastic, anytime. I smiled, remembering her at the sink, paisley apron round her waist, washing her array of plastic flowers, using an old toothbrush to get in between the gaudy coloured petals.

It was nine-twenty a.m. as I stepped into the front room of the bungalow. Her black coat was still slumped over the arm of the red and green settee. Her red purse, bus pass face-up, was sticking out from under one of the cushions. A half-empty bottle of olive oil stood next to a hairbrush still misted with strands of her white hair. On the sideboard, alongside an old, faded prayer book, various coins, a picture of ten-year-old me in a black leather jacket with a white stripe across the chest. Black hair plastered down, my smile showing the gap between my teeth that I could fit a half-crown in. There were picturesque Christmas and birthday cards on the wall in plastic frames. I walked around, remembering each one, and the way she used to fill her tiny front room with old Christmas cards going back to just after the war. The dish of water she swore kept away sore throats still sat next to the two-bar electric fire. Hand-sewn, homemade knickers, skirts, blouses and tea towels straggled over the rods of her clothes rack, hanging a foot from the kitchen ceiling.

I stood at the door of her walk-in larder, recalling the conversations we had had about the advantages of a fridge. She wouldn't budge. It was her way, and that's how she wanted it to stay. The marble slab for her meats. The damp tea towel for keeping bread fresh, and the various enamel basins she used for steeping peas and pulses. On the kitchenette table, alongside her tea strainer, was her single cup and saucer next to my 'I love Mum' mug.

I went into the bedroom. Through the half-closed curtains, a yellow oblong of sunlight slid over the bedroom carpet. The forty-watt bulb made no real difference to the light. There was a whiff of Lifebuoy soap mingled with the smell of hospital. There were boxes of bandages, surgical stockings, and enough medicines to open a chemist's. A pair of clogs underneath a mahogany wardrobe stood next to a pair of sandals and a pair of flat walking-out shoes. The walls were white, bare, except for a small black crucifix. The bed had been made. I smiled, thinking of the times she had shouted to me, 'I can't leave the house without making the bed. What will they say if someone breaks in!' I remembered her waxed face when I first saw her dead. The undignified way her head had fallen back, mouth open, cheeks sucked in. She would have hated it.

Alone in Mum's bedroom, I reread her obituary in the local paper—'*Street, Kitty (née O'Mara), aged eighty-two, passed 25th March 1996...*'—then put it back on the polished surface of the dressing table. I opened the drawer she had called the 'special one', though it had never been a secret. I had always known what was in it. We had been through it so many times, mother and son together, on rainy days. Between thumb and forefinger, the way she used to, I clicked open her black and gold compact, dabbed some powder on my hand, smelt it, then rubbed it over the side of her face as I used to do for her all those years ago. I flicked the rest of the vanilla-smelling powder onto the bed.

From the drawer I lifted out a large envelope tied with a white silk band. There was a certificate recording her marriage to Thomas Edgar Street in 1952. And Dad's death certificate, 1976. There was also a black and white photograph of myself, a small boy of six, holding my mother's hand in front of the windmill at Haigh Hall, Aspull, beside the lane she walked with the other single mums. I was trying to remember the moment and who might have been holding the camera.

I carefully brushed her thin lips with her favourite bright red lipstick, careful not to smudge. Then, leaning over her, I lightly powered her nose to hide the many freckles she had hated for as long as I could remember. I gently combed her hair, feeling every white strand sliding through her blue comb, and tucked some behind her ears, the way she herself did whenever she had to meet someone. She would tuck it back ever so gently, almost flirtatious. I fiddled with the collar of her nightie: straight, neat. Moisturised her hands with Ponds Cold Cream. She would have liked all of it. Being made presentable for the undertakers.

I squeezed her hand and tasted my last kiss, watching the pain of several lifetimes drain from her eighty-two-year-old face. I took the dark blue bottle of 'Evening in Paris', from the walnut dressing table Social Services had given her, lifted the tiny gold lid and dabbed it on her wrist, the way she used to. It had been empty for as long as I could remember.

GOALKEEPER IS AVAILABLE IN
PAPERBACK, E-BOOK AND KINDLE

Enjoyed reading this book? Please support our work by leaving a review and/or rating at Goodreads.com, Amazon, and wherever you purchased this copy.

SPONDYLUX PRESS

An inclusive independent publisher of own-voice stories, set up and run by autistic professionals to promote neurodiversity, sustainability, social change and justice.

www.SpondyluxPress.com

@SpondyluxPress